GUIDE TO FIRST-YEAR

Writing

Second Edition

Dr. Lynée Gaillet, Director
Dr. Angela Hall-Godsey, Associate Director
Jennifer L. Vala, Assistant Director

Georgia State University

Lower Division Studies

FOUNTAINHEAD
PRESS

As a textbook publisher, we are faced with enormous environmental issues due the large amount of paper contained in our print products. Since our inception in 2002, we have worked diligently to be as eco-friendly as possible.

Our "green" initiatives include:

Electronic Products
We deliver products in non-paper form whenever possible. This includes pdf down-loadables, flash drives, & CD's.

Electronic Samples
We use a new electronic sampling system, called Xample. Instructor samples are sent via a personalized web page that links to pdf downloads.

FSC Certified Printers
All of our Printers are certified by the Forest Service Council which promotes envi-ronmentally and socially responsible management of the world's forests. This pro-gram allows consumer groups, individual consumers and businesses to work together hand in hand to promote responsible use of the world's forests as a renewable and sustainable resource.

Recycled Paper
Almost all of our products are printed on a minimum of 10-30% post consumer waste recycled paper.

Support of Green Causes
When we do print, we donate a portion of our revenue to Green causes. Listed below are a few of the organizations that have received donations from Fountain-head Press. We welcome your feedback and suggestions for contributions, as we are always searching for worthy initiatives.
Rainforest 2 Reef
Environmental Working Group

Cover Designer: Doris Bruey
Book Layout: OffCenter Concept House

Books may be purchased for educational purpose.

For information, please call or write:

1-800-586-0030

Fountainhead Press
Southlake, TX 76092

Web site: www.fountainheadpress.com

Email: customerservice@fountainheadpress.com

ISBN: 978-1-59871-693-1

Printed in the United States of America

Contents

Acknowledgments

The *Guide to First-Year Writing,* 2nd edition is the product of hard work by faculty, staff, and teachers in the Lower Division Studies program of the Department of English at Georgia State University. In addition to authoring this text, participants on various committees gathered information, organized essays and art submissions, as well as conducted several rounds of student and faculty-centered surveys. The feedback from instructors and students was instrumental in creating the second edition of the *Guide to First-Year Writing.*

Editors

General Editor
Lynée Lewis Gaillet, Ph.D.

Managing and Contributing Editor
Angela Hall-Godsey, Ph.D.

Contributing Editor
Jennifer L. Vala

Editorial Staff
Helen Cauley
Tara Causey
Donald Gammill
Marta Hess
Shane McGowan
Zachary Rearick
Stephanie Rountree
Lara Smith-Sitton
Ellen Stockstill
Jessica Temple
Lelania Ottobani Watkins

Student Art Contributors

Courtney Anderson, Alesa Barron, Michael Black-Akert, Melinda Childs, Lorelei Crystalilly Marden, Charles Clark, Nadia Deljou, Patrick Duffy, Marissa Graziano, Judith Kim, Stephanie Liebetreu, Shedaria Presley, Nadia Quyyum, Courtney Jane Richir, Mark Alan Ross, Joshua Sheridan, Liana Snead, James Supreme, Fenton Thompson, Lillia Tran, Jiri Vala Jr., William Walsh, Teal Waxelbaum, Joshua Yu

Student Writing Contributors

Deranda B., Jocelyn Lopez, Jessica Martinez, Blake Pilgrim

Cover Photo

"Holi – Festival of Colors 2" by Joshua Yu

"Courtyard" by Patrick Duffy

Introduction to Lower Division Studies and First-Year Writing Classes

WHAT IS LOWER DIVISION STUDIES?

By now you have attended several orientation programs introducing you to university life. As a first-year student, you are probably excited to start on this path toward your degree. The Lower Division Studies program for the Department of English welcomes you to Georgia State University. Our program comprises all first and second year composition (English 1101, English 1102, and English 1103) and literature courses (English 2110, 2120, and 2130). Our directors and staff oversee the pedagogical design and curriculum for all of these courses. In addition to this work, our program trains and supports all instructors who teach 1000 and 2000 level English courses. Since every student must complete first-year writing courses (part of the University's CORE classes), our program seeks to provide assistance and direction to over three thousand students a semester. One way we manage contact with so many students is by creating a centralized location for Lower Division information – the Lower Division Office, which is housed in the English Department. Another way we monitor the progress of our first-year students is through the creation of this textbook and companion website for use in all composition courses. The material you learn in these introductory courses will serve as the foundation of your academic pursuits. We encourage you to become familiar with Lower Division Studies (LDS).

Lower Division Studies Administration

Dr. Lynée Lewis Gaillet, Director, Lower Division Studies
lgaillet@gsu.edu

Dr. Angela Hall-Godsey, Associate Director, Lower Division Studies
ahallgodsey1@gsu.edu

Jennifer L. Vala, Assistant Director, Lower Division Studies
jvala1@gsu.edu

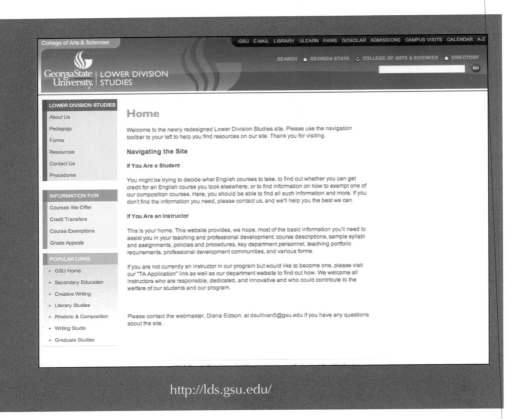

http://lds.gsu.edu/

Web Resources

Lower Division Studies maintains its own webpage, which houses valuable administrative information. To visit this site, go to http://www.english.gsu.edu/~lds/

Guide to First Year Writing also has a companion site, which is a good place to find supplemental leaning resources. Please visit this site to search for information on the *Guide*, writing tutorials, links to educational resources, grammar tutorials, and sample student essays. The site also posts Lower Division Policy information pertinent to GSU students. To visit this site, go to http://www.guidetowriting.gsu.edu

WHY DO I HAVE TO TAKE A WRITING CLASS?

Regardless of your major and intended career path, all students and professionals must know how to write well. Simply conducting scientific experiments won't cut it – you will need to know how to appropriately and

effectively articulate your findings. Most college classes require writing as one of the ways instructors assess what you know. So, English courses are not the *only* courses that require writing. More pointedly, writing involves critical thinking. Those who learn how to write well must also learn valuable skills in reading comprehension, synthesizing, argumentation, rhetorical analysis, and organization. As you learn how to write better, you will also learn how to articulate your point of view, develop clear and ethically-driven arguments, and how to become stronger *thinkers*. As a critical thinker, your role as a student, and later as a professional, strengthens. In addition your participation in a university community and your ability to articulate your experiences can also benefit your outside and personal interests.

What kind of writing do you imagine you will do as a professional in the work force? Perhaps you think you won't have to really "write" anything

"Lord of the Arts" by Joshua Sheridan

given your major; however, you may be surprised by the amount of writing required in most professions. The College Board's National Commission on Writing compiled a report representing responses from over 100 corporate leaders of American companies. This report, "Writing A Ticket to Work … Or a Ticket Out: A Survey of Business Leaders," outlines the expectations those in the corporate world have about employee writing competencies. The research found that writing is not only a "threshold skill of employment and promotion, particularly among salaried employees," but that two-thirds of all salaried employees in industry has some writing responsibility" (3). Of course, a published report shouldn't be the only evidence to convince you of the benefit of effective writing skills. Have you ever sent an email to a coworker, teacher, or family member that didn't "say" what you wanted it to mean? In every job, regardless of the industry, you will need to write *something*: including, memos, emails, proposals, reports, formal findings analysis, and summaries of company materials. Research suggests that those who write better are more hirable, marketable, and promotable.

WHAT HAPPENS IN A WRITING CLASS?

Georgia State University's composition courses are capped at 25 students per class, which allows more direct and individual classroom instruction. Instead of sitting in a lecture hall taking notes with one hundred other students, you will engage with the writing process through what's known as active and student-centered learning. What are these modes of learning? Well, your class may involve in-class writing assignments, oral presentations, classroom debates, community-driven assignments, peer editing, and group projects. The classroom becomes a community of writers, who are all interested in developing modes of written expression. As a first-year composition student, you will be expected to engage in classroom discussions, to complete reading and writing assignments

"The Art of Writing" by Alesa Barron

outside of class, and to participate in the editing process for your papers and papers written by your peers.

Think of the writing classroom as a space where you *learn* how to write and *write* in order to learn. The writing class invites inquiry and offers instruction for processing your initial queries and articulating your findings. In addition to learning how to write better, your instructor will help you improve your self-expression and refine your abilities to research, reflect, read actively, organize findings, and express critiques.

Composition courses are more than mere *grammar* courses.   Correct grammar and mechanics are fundamental to developing clear writing and to illustrating credibility for your audience. However, effective compositing involves logic, organization, research support, and consideration of the rhetorical situation in addition to correct grammar usage.   The task for your next semester will be to assess your writing weaknesses (as well as your strengths) and work on demonstrating scholarly writing skills. Your instructors are trained to help you through this process.   So, be sure you become familiar with the classroom rules, the course expectations, and ways in which you can improve your writing by visiting your instructor during office hours and making appointments with a Writing Studio tutor: http://www.writingstudio.gsu.edu/.

One

Invention and Process

Many first-year college writers who attempt to sit down and compose the first draft of an assignment soon find themselves frustrated because they don't know what to say. For many experienced writers, the writing process consists of four stages: pre-writing, drafting, revising, and editing—although these composing tasks rarely occur linearly. Writers usually jump back and forth from one stage to another within the writing process. In this chapter, we will define each of these recursive stages in the writing process in hopes that understanding how you write best will make composing easier.

First, consider where you write. What type of environment is necessary for both focus and inspiration? Do you need to work in a quiet place without distractions, like the library? Do you need a cup of coffee or a snack before you sit down to write? Do you find that you work best when you are near a window or outside? What role does electronic communication/internet access have on your writing environment? Do you work better when you are fully "plugged in," or do you find it easier to write without the distractions of the Web or a phone?

In *The Courage to Write*, author Ralph Keyes explains that noted novelist and short-story writer John Cheever made a habit of donning a suit and tie each morning, walking downstairs to his basement, placing his suit on a hanger, and then writing all day in his underwear. In a 1989 interview with the British Broadcasting Corporation, famous African American writer Maya Angelou explained that for years she would wake up at five in the morning and check into a hotel room. Once there, she would lie on the bed with a bottle of sherry, a deck of cards, a Roget's Thesaurus, and a Bible, and would then proceed to write on a legal pad until the afternoon, producing approximately 10–12 pages of material, which she would later edit down to only three or four pages.

Not all writers have such interesting or specific writing environments; however, it is important to be aware of where and how you work best. Keep in mind that sometimes, changing the writing environment can help you find what Chickasaw writer Linda Hogan refers to as the writing "zone," or the "heart of it"—the place where your ideas begin to flow.

PRE-WRITING

Pre-Writing, which usually includes some combination of thinking and writing, involves all the things that you do before you actually start to write the draft of your composition. You've probably heard of pre-writing before, as most high school composition teachers emphasize several of these pre-writing strategies. Unfortunately, students often skip this important step, viewing it as "extra work," and then proceed to dive headlong into writing a paper. Years of composition research strongly suggest that prewriting strategies make writing easier and better. Skip this step, and the finished product will suffer. Ten minutes of prewriting can do wonders, even if only some of your pre-writing thoughts end up in the final draft. Prewriting can generate good ideas about both content and structure, and, perhaps even more importantly, can ward off the desperate, anxiety-ridden feeling of writer's block.

The following prewriting techniques are suggestions that often yield quality writing; they are not, however, hard-and-fast rules—different strategies work for different people, and it is important to try various methods to find what works best for you. Consider these twwo tips: 1. Read the assignment thoroughly. 2. Begin these pre-writing strategies the day a paper is assigned; do not wait to start the process the night before a draft is due.

Thinking about the Topic

The generative process of writing (i.e. getting ideas about what to say) begins long before a writer sits down at a computer. Writers use free moments to think about what they are going to write, whether they are in the shower, the car, or walking to school or work. Professional writers report that many of their best ideas come to them during these "down" times, and a number of these writers keep a notebook handy to record their ideas. This practice wards off the anxiety of facing a blank screen and writer's block.

Talking about the Topic

Brainstorm ideas with a friend, a pen, and a notebook. Talking out ideas with another person forces a writer to pull ideas into a coherent form. A listener can tell a writer whether or not an idea makes sense, or if additional ideas and perspectives should be considered. This strategy also helps a writer identify the *purpose* of and the *audience* for the composition—two of the most important elements of powerful, successful writing, both in college and beyond. In addition to working with a friend, you may also find it helpful to work with the tutors at the Georgia State University Writing Studio, all of whom can help you generate good ideas for your assignments. The Writing Studio tutors are well-versed in all steps of the writing process, and many students find it advantageous to make appointments at the Writing Studio during each stage of an assignment.

"Flying Ideas" by Lillia Tran

Free Association or Brainstorming

A *heuristic* is a technique that prompts a writer's memories and ideas. Brainstorming—listing anything and everything that comes to mind about a topic—is familiar to most students. For more fruitful results, take brainstorming a step further: pick out specific words or phrases from your initial brainstorm and engage in a secondary brainstorm (or looping) of these narrowed ideas. These techniques can help you to generate ideas on virtually any topic and help you come up with a thesis and outline. On the other hand, these techniques might also provide new or different directions for your topic than what you may have been initially considering. Not all ideas listed will be relevant, but brainstorming provides an excellent starting point.

Freewriting

Putting pen to paper (or fingers to the keyboard), writers "freewrite" anything that comes to mind on a topic for at least 10 minutes, without stopping the movement of the pen or keys--and without worrying about grammar, spelling, or punctuation. This technique does wonders to eliminate the stress of the first draft. Authors write the topic at the top of the page to keep focused, yet they must feel free to include extraneous material, as they are writing whatever drifts across their mind (for example: "I'm not sure what she wants, I can't think of anything, this is dumb this is dumb ...."). Don't worry; at some point, on-topic ideas will appear. Just as athletes must warm up before practice or competition, writers must "warm up" their cognitive and emotional processes in order to write at peak performance.

Cubing

This heuristic envisions a cube, which has six sides, to prompt thinking on multiple sides of a topic. Cubing entails the following steps: 1. Describe the topic or argument. 2. Compare it to other topics or arguments. 3. Free associate (brainstorm) on the topic or argument. 4. Analyze the topic or argument: How is it significant? How does it work? 5. Argue *for* or *against* any part of the topic or argument, or state your personal position concisely. 6. Ask what are the real-life ramifications of this topic or argument? Why should an audience care about this topic? By writing either a little or a lot on each section, writers force themselves to see a topic from multiple angles and in the process, generate new ideas.

Questions and Answers

Writers often think of questions that they (or others) may pose about a topic. Writers then try to answer those questions, sometimes enlisting the help of a friend to assist in this activity. Like freewriting, this strategy is not concerned with grammar or spelling; instead, it simply helps writers develop ideas and arguments. When writers answer questions, they practice explaining concepts—and building effective arguments—in their own words.

The Five W's and an H: Basic Questions of Journalism

Ask (and then try to answer) the basic questions a journalist would ask: Who? What? When? Where? Why? How? These questions will help you find main points needed for expository or persuasive writing. Asking questions not only helps generate ideas, but can also help narrow the focus of a composition, aiding in the formulation of a specific argument.

Diving into General Research

Most people would agree that it is easier to write about a familiar topic than an unfamiliar one. Whether your instructor assigns a topic that is completely foreign to you or allows you to select your topic, you may still have problems ascertaining the general "lay of the land" of that topic—the geography of its issues and controversies. (Tip: Ask a librarian about the site "Issues and Controversies," available through GSU's Pullen Library). Diving into general research may provide the background needed to formulate an effective argument that will result in a successful composition. Rather than struggling to form a well-thought-out thesis statement in the beginning, you can instead begin general research on your topic, and an interesting argument may emerge during this process. See Chapter Four: Research and Documentation for ways to begin this valuable pre-writing method.

▬ DRAFTING

After taking the time to pre-write and jot down potential thoughts and connections related to your topic, begin organizing your ideas in a sequence that will clearly relay both the *purpose* of the composition as well as the appeal to your *audience*. This part of the writing process is typically called "drafting." Remember, everyone writes differently; as with the other parts of the writing process, this component also varies from writer to writer. Some people compose body paragraphs first and then tackle the introduction. Some ignore spelling and grammar in a first draft—they go with the flow of their ideas and save the fine-tuning for later (this is good advice for any writer). Regardless of the order in which you create all the necessary parts of your composition, a solid first draft should have a specific focus, an organizational strategy, an introduction, body paragraphs that support the composition's focus, and a conclusion. Once you have each part, you can begin to rework everything you've written to make it stronger and more cohesive. Keep in mind that writing is a recursive process, meaning that it doesn't always follow a linear progression from start to finish. Therefore, be prepared for early drafts to be messy.

REVISION: THE ART OF "RE-SEEING" WRITING

Revision, the final major component of the writing process, centers on the aforementioned "re-working" of your draft so that your composition can reach its full potential. Revision takes a high priority in all writing courses. Yes, it takes time and effort, but the effort a writer puts into revising his or her work always proves worth the effort in the end. Done well, revision results in clearer, stronger, and more effective writing, as well as a more interesting reading experience for the audience.

So what exactly is revision and how do you do it? Revision is not editing, and it is not proofreading. Ideally, these tasks come later in the writing process. Revision involves much more than running SpellCheck and adjusting a comma here and there. Rather, it involves a wholesale re-seeing of the entire paper. Revision may include re-thinking the style and tone, or rearranging the structure (i.e. re-ordering the content). The following three levels of revision may occur and recur at any stage in the writing process. Once again, there is no mandatory order to any stage of the writing process.

The Organizational Level

The organization of a composition enables the reader to follow along and understand the connections between ideas and how those ideas relate back to the composition's main focus. Here are a few questions that might help you think critically about your organization: Does the paper progress logically from beginning to end? Where might readers get bogged down, get lost, or lose interest? Does the thesis statement echo in every sentence of the paper, or can sentences or entire paragraphs be cut completely? Does the paper contain transitions, guiding the reader smoothly among paragraphs and sections, or does it jump around, jarring the reader?

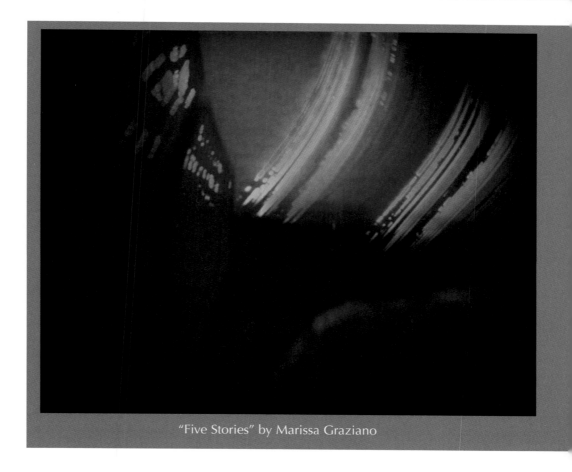

"Five Stories" by Marissa Graziano

Take a look at the following introduction and initial sentences of the first body paragraph from a Georgia State student's essay. Pay particular attention to how the thesis statement outlines the main points that will be discussed in the essay and how the topic sentence of the first body paragraph re-states the first main point from the thesis.

Anahita Mahmoudabadi
Instructor D'Cruze
English 1102
5 March 2013

Limitations on the "Superhighway" of Information

The Internet, also known as the "Superhighway" of information, drastically changes the way information is distributed (Strickland). It connects individuals worldwide and opens the lines of communication; however, it may also expose users to unsuitable and harmful content. Since there are potential dangers of the Internet, censorship of the Internet has become prevalent and varies from country-to-country. On-line censorship can be defined as the control of what is distributed or viewed on the Internet through licensing agreements, password protected sites, and site moderators who flag and edit materials posted by users. The issue of censorship is becoming increasingly important as a result ever-changing and constant new developments of communication technology and because of the rise of social networking sites. **Overall, censorship of the Internet is beneficial to society because it protects children from unsuitable content, prevents the display of disrespectful content to a particular individual or community, and protects national security.**

The Internet exposes content that is not suitable for the entire public, especially minors. Even if children aren't looking for porn, it will find them, through spam mail and pop-up ads featured on many websites. Simple and innocent keyword searches can often lead minors to sexually inappropriate sites, even if their intention was not to search for the explicit material.

The Content Level

Consider questions like: Does the paper make sense? Will it spark audience interest from the very first sentence? Is it informative? Does it say something unique, or does it feel like a rehash? Does its thesis—its main idea or argument—come through in a crystal-clear manner to its intended audience? Does strong evidence back up every point? Does any background information or do any technical terms need brief explanation? Does the paper cite sources responsibly?

The Style Level

Writers develop their individual styles through practice as they experiment with different ways of expressing themselves. Many elements of writing contribute to individual style. These elements include varying the lengths of sentences, making specific and precise word choices, using repetition effectively, varying sentence structure, and using the appropriate active or passive voices. As writers gain experience in their craft, they become better at identifying and enhancing their styles and finding their own authentic, unique voices. Reading experienced writers' work and studying the ways in which they express their ideas also help you develop your individual style.

The following sample paragraphs show the difference in prose (writing) between a first-draft and a revision. Notice how the prose in the revised paragraph is smoother and more interesting.

"Kana" by Liana Sneed

First Draft:

The Sweet Auburn Curb Market in Atlanta is a very interesting place. Many vendors from all over the city sell meat, vegetables, and other food. Restaurants provide lots of choices. The first thing you notice when you go to the Auburn Market is the smell of many kinds of food. Another thing you should notice in the market is the space itself. The floors are bare and it is very industrial looking. There are many things that are interesting about the market, including the variety of vendors. There is a Caribbean restaurant, a popcorn shop that sells over one hundred varieties, a bakery, and businesses selling everything from fresh seafood to cows' ears. Other businesses include a flower shop, a pharmacy, a bookstore and a convenience store. There is something for everyone at the Sweet Auburn Curb Market.

Revised Draft:

At the Sweet Auburn Curb Market shoppers and browsers alike can experience one of the most interesting places in Atlanta. At first glance, visitors notice the industrial appearance of the building with its cement floors and bare walls. Soon, however, the delicious aromas of different cuisines entice shoppers to explore the wide variety of food vendors who offer selections from fresh seafood to cows' ears, and provide something for every taste. Hungry visitors can satisfy their appetites at restaurants specializing in Caribbean food, baked goods, and even popcorn in over one hundred varieties. Other businesses include a flower shop, pharmacy, bookstore, and convenience store, making the market an ideal place for all shoppers' needs. The Sweet Auburn Curb Market has something for everyone to enjoy.

Peer Response: Getting a Second Opinion

Experienced writers frequently discuss their ideas and compositions with other writers in order to "test drive" their work. Professional writers even have their own paid editors, which indicates just how important it is to have someone else read and comment on your work.

Due to the vital nature of having "a different set of eyes" look at your work, your composition instructor may ask you to participate in a peer review assignment. This activity, which might be conducted in or out of class, will give you and your classmates the opportunity to read, assess, ask questions about, and make suggestions to improve each other's writing. Your instructor might ask you to bring either a partial draft or a completed essay for review; however, regardless of what he or she requires, you will only receive the full benefit of the process by jumping in with both feet and following your instructors guidelines for peer review.

No matter what suggestions your peer offers, remember that your writing ultimately belongs to you and you are responsible for any changes you make.

Calling on Creativity: New Directions in Revision

As we have seen, revision literally means re-visioning a paper through a new set of eyes. Ideally, revision should include both the writer's and an editor's perspectives, and perhaps the views of a peer response group, as well. Keep in mind that the following revision strategies are not employed all at once. "Stuck" writers, perhaps dissatisfied with a draft, can apply one or more of the following techniques within their specific assignment guidelines to get the process moving:

1. Write a new introduction
2. Write a new conclusion
3. Switch the point of view (from first-person to third-person or from third-person to first-person)
4. Add dialogue to the description of an event
5. Re-write the conclusion as an introduction, and then write a new conclusion
6. Write a dialogue with a friend describing the paper, explaining why the topic matters, and specific points of importance
7. Create a stream-of-consciousness freewrite about what is going on beneath the surface of the action, arguments, or explanations
8. Describe a place alluded to in the paper using all five senses
9. Open by starting in the middle of the action
10. Describe a person mentioned in the paper
11. Tell what happens after the paper ends
12. Describe what happened before the events of the paper
13. Describe a personal experience related to an argument in the paper
14. Argue from the opposite point of view
15. Create a dialogue representing two or more points of view

16. Write an argument as a narrative
17. Write an analysis as a letter to a friend
18. Write an argument as a stream-of-consciousness freewrite
19. Write to a different audience—GSU's president, your roommate, a grandmother
20. Write a formal argument as a poem
21. Put the draft aside and write a quick outline of the points *you* want to make
22. Use color coding: Write down the important points of the paper, assigning each a color. Then, color code each sentence in the paper based on the point to which it corresponds. If the paper looks like a rainbow, or if randomly-colored sentences appear in one paragraph (or if sentences with *no* color appear), then rework the structure of the paper.

A Revision Checklist for Strong, Effective Writing

Purpose
- Did I follow the assignment guidelines?
- Did I make my purpose clear to the reader?
- Are audience, purpose, and content appropriate and effective?

Audience
- Does the paper effectively engage my audience?
- Does it appeal to my audience's logic and/or emotions?
- Does it establish my *ethos* as a writer (will the audience find my authorial persona reliable and trustworthy)?

Focus
- Is the thesis (main idea) clear, strong, and specific?
- Does every paragraph and idea relate to the thesis?
- Does the paper include irrelevant points? What can be cut to make the paper tighter and stronger?

Ideas
- Did I say what I wanted to say?
- Am I missing any important ideas?
- Did I include strong evidence to effectively state my point? Did I provide enough examples?
- Does the paper answer the "So What" question—"Why does this matter?"

Organization

- How can the introduction better engage the reader, establish the tone, and/or set up the main idea of the paper?
- Can I cut the phrase, "In conclusion," and make the ending more sophisticated? Does the ending grab attention, giving readers something to carry away?

Structure

- Does the information unfold in the most effective order?
- Does the essay lead the reader through the essay in a clear and logical way?

Paragraphs and Transitions

- Does each paragraph focus on one main point, relevant to the thesis of the paper?
- Do I provide smooth transitions between paragraphs?
- Does each sentence connect to the one that came before it and the one that follows? Or does the writing feel disjointed?

Tone and Style

- Does the piece speak with a tone and writing style consistent and appropriate for subject, purpose, and audience?

Sentence Structure

- Does each sentence on its own make sense?
- Are sentences well-constructed, effective, and varied?
- Are there too many short, choppy sentences? Too many long, wordy sentences? Can these be juxtaposed to make reading more interesting?

Grammar and Spelling

- Did I consult my composition handbook on use of commas and other points unclear to me?
- Did I not only run SpellCheck, but also look at *every single word* in the essay to ensure correct usage?

Citation of Sources

- Does the paper use the assigned style (most likely MLA in first-year writing classes)?
- Does the paper cite outside sources correctly within the text?

- Does the paper end with a properly formatted Works Cited page, including all outside sources? Do any sources appear on Works Cited page that are *not* cited within the paper?

EDITING

Editing, the final major step in the writing process, sometimes seems very similar to revision; however, it is distinct in one significant way: whereas revision encompasses "re-seeing" the composition as a whole, editing takes a closer look at the individual paragraphs, sentences, and words that make up the work. Editing often comes at the end of the writing process for a number of good reasons. Efficient writers do not spend time fixing punctuation in a paragraph they might eliminate later. A proven editing technique for catching structural and sentence-level errors is to read the paper *out loud,* and slowly. Some writers read their papers backwards, starting with the last sentence, and focus on just one element at a time (such as spelling or punctuation). If editing the entire paper nonstop proves overwhelming, a writer may read aloud and edit one paragraph at a time. Editing need not occur in one sitting; some writers focus on one page, and then take a break.

No matter how you conduct your editing process, this is the time to ask yourself if incorrect grammar, punctuation, or spelling might prevent readers from making sense of what you have written. Also challenge yourself with editing inquiries involving style and tone: Will readers stumble over awkward phrasing, or be bored by redundancies or excessive repetition? Will the words you use convey a confident, level-headed tone, or does an obnoxious, arrogant attitude come across instead? The editing process may seem tedious and solely concerned with small things, but as the famous 19th century author Mark Twain once said, "The difference between the almost right word and the right word is really a large matter—it's the difference between the lightning bug and the lightning."

Technology makes editing easier. With programs such as SpellCheck, writers can quickly spot misspelled words and grammatical inconsistencies. However, they neglect to explain exactly why an error is incorrect. In short, take these electronic recommendations with the proverbial grain of salt; as yet, no digital logic can effectively substitute for the skilled eye of a careful, knowledgeable editor.

To help you avoid the most common editing pitfalls, below you will find a brief review of some persistent writing errors, with corresponding advice.

"Hyperbolic" by Mark Alan Ross

GRAMMAR RULES FOR REVIEW

Punctuation: Commas

Misuse of commas consistently ranks among the top punctuation errors. While commas serve a variety of purposes, here are a few of the most frequent ways to use them to make your writing clearer.

1. Add a comma before a coordinating conjunction that joins two independent clauses

Do you remember the FANBOYS (for, and, nor, but, or yet, so)? These coordinating conjunctions link two complete sentences (independent clauses). To be a complete sentence, there must be a subject and a verb:

I wanted to go to the beach.

I couldn't get the time off from work.

Using a comma and a conjunction, the two can be connected to form one compound sentence:

I wanted to go to the beach, but I couldn't get the time off from work.

The comma, placed just before the conjunction, signals the move from one complete clause to the next.

Note that the subject of both sentences is *I*. In that case, the writer might want to combine the two clauses into one sentence with the same subject:

I wanted to go to the beach but couldn't get the time off from work.

In this instance, no comma is needed before the conjunction, since what follows is not a complete sentence (*couldn't get the time off from work*). Both verbs – *wanted* and *couldn't get* – have the same subject, so they are no longer two independent clauses.

2. Add a conjunction with a comma between two complete sentences.

When two complete sentences (independent clauses with their own subjects and verbs) are connected with a comma, but not with a conjunction, the result is known as a comma splice error. To determine if these are, in fact, two complete sentences, try substituting a period instead of a comma:

This, semester, I plan to join the marching band.

I will attend every football game.

If the period indicates that there are, in fact, two distinct sentences, then joining them with a comma will require a coordinating conjunction (FAN-BOYS):

This semester, I plan to join the marching band, and I will attend every football game.

3. Use a comma to set off an introductory phrase

The backbone of a sentence is its subject and its verb. These two elements often carry the weight of meaning, which is why strong verbs with subjects who perform the verb's action often form the most effective sentences.

Susan swims at the GSU pool.

The subject, *Susan*, performs the action of the verb, *swims*, in a sentence with a clear meaning. But what if the writer wants to embellish a bit? Adding an introductory phrase can provide detail that enhances the sentence but is not part of the main structure, so it is set apart by a comma:

After running on the treadmill, Susan swims at the GSU pool.

Commas also offset introductory words such as *however, furthermore,* and *in addition*.

> *In addition, she enjoys lifting weights.*

4. Use commas to set off nonessential/essential information

Commas are used before and after words that interrupt a sentence to add extra information. If those additional words do not affect the basic meaning of the sentence, then they are considered "extra," and are set off by commas.

> *My friend, who has red hair, left her iPad in the classroom.*

However, if the red hair is a distinguishing characteristic that specifically identifies which friend is being discussed, then it is key to the meaning of the sentence and does not require commas:

> *My friend who has red hair left her iPad in the classroom.*

Consider these examples as well:

> *The student who won the writing contest is in our class.*

Without commas, the reader understands that the specific student being discussed is not just any member of the class, but the person who won the contest. Compare that to:

> *The student, who won the writing contest, is in our class.*

Here, the student in the class happens to be the person who won a writing contest, but that information is not necessary to distinguish one student from another.

Punctuation: Semicolons

Semicolons serve different purposes, but in each case, the goal is to help the reader follow the direction and meaning of the sentence.

1. Use a semicolon to join two independent clauses that are closely related.

Two complete sentences that share a link in meaning can be joined by inserting a semicolon between the two. While they would be fine standing on their own, the semicolon indicates to the reader that there is a special connection between the two.

You should enroll in a history class; you have always had an interest in that subject.

Semicolons often precede words that indicate a transition: however, therefore, moreover, furthermore, nevertheless.

You should enroll in a history class; however, all the sections for fall are full.

2. **Use a semicolon to separate items in a list that already includes commas.**

When writing a long list that may already include items with commas, use semicolons to help the reader follow the sequence.

The meeting was attended by Dr. Becker, the university president; Dr. Palms, the provost; and Dr. Stout, the dean of students.

Punctuation: Colons

A colon is used after a complete sentence to introduce a word, phrase, clause, list, or quotation. It indicates that what follows proves or explains the sentence before the colon.

Students choose GSU for three reasons: its urban environment, its diverse population, and its outstanding academic reputation.

Vague Pronoun Reference/Pronoun Agreement

One of the most frequent ways writers throw readers off track is by creating confusion with pronouns. To be as clear as possible, you must be certain that a specific noun precedes a pronoun, so the reader knows exactly who or what is being discussed. For example:

My classmates are going to see a play. We intend to carpool to the theater.

By initially establishing that *the classmates* are doing something, the reader can easily make the connection to the pronoun *we*. But it's not quite as obvious when there are two nouns involved:

Georgia State has a great football team! It is nationally ranked.

In this case, the reader can easily be confused as to whether the *it* pronoun refers to Georgia State or the football team.

Confusion can also arise with the possessive pronoun *their*. While *my, your, ours,* and *his/hers* clearly connect to *I, you, we,* and *him/her, their* is often mistakenly used as a "default" possessive for singular and plural pronouns. Remember that *their* goes with *they*:

> *The students submitted their papers on the last day of class.*

If there is only one student, use a singular possessive pronoun:

> *The student submitted her paper on the last day of class.*

It's also worth noting that, in most cases, *their* will precede a plural noun, unless the writer specifically means that more than one person shares ownership:

> *My parents have owned their house since 2010.*

In this sentence, the plural *their* relates to the plural *parents* who own one house together.

Misplaced Modifier

A modifier is a word, phrase or clause that describes something. To avoid reader confusion, the modifier works best when it is placed next to the item it is describing. For instance, consider this sentence:

> *Kate ate a sandwich wearing a GSU sweatshirt.*

Since *sandwich* precedes *wearing a GSU sweatshirt*, it appears that Kate's snack was well-dressed. In fact, the writer meant to say:

> *Kate, wearing a GSU sweatshirt, ate a sandwich.*

Another common problem with modifiers happens when they appear at the beginning of a sentence. Writers are fond of starting off with phrases such as *walking to class, while listening to the podcast, driving by the scene of the accident,* etc. But take note: When using an opening phrase that includes an *–ing* verb, the person performing the action of that verb needs to be the subject that comes next:

> *Walking to class, Sam met several of his friends.*

Here, it's clear that Sam was doing the walking when he met his friends. Likewise:

> *While listening to the podcast, the class was busy taking notes on important points.*

The class is the one doing the listening. But occasionally, a writer will use a different subject after the clause, creating a sentence like this:

> *Walking down the street, a car jumped the curb and hit me.*

Since *car* is the subject, it appears the car was doing the walking. A clearer version might read as one of these:

> *Speeding down the street, a car jumped the curb and hit me.*

> *While I was walking down the street, a car jumped the curb and hit me.*

Parallel Structure

There are many times when a writer wants to elaborate and relate significant ideas. For instance:

> *Biology is my major because it is challenging, interesting, and exciting.*

In this case, the writer is sharing enthusiasm for the subject *biology* by identifying it with three adjectives: *challenging, interesting, and exciting.* Each of those adjectives on its own could complete the phrase: *Biology is my major because it is…* This alignment of multiple words (or phrases) that link to one noun or verb is called parallel structure. In the example above, all of the elements that describe *biology* are parallel since they are all adjectives.

Many times, writers begin a parallel construction only to lose their way before the end of the sentence. Consider this example:

> *Biology is my major because it is challenging, interesting, and I plan to be a veterinarian.*

The writer begins by describing her major with the adjectives *challenging and interesting*, but then veers into another complete sentence – *I plan to be a veterinarian* – which breaks the parallel structure. A possible solution to this problem is:

> *Biology is my major because it is challenging and interesting, and I plan to be a veterinarian.*

Fragments

A fragment is an incomplete sentence. It may be a phrase without a subject or verb, or it may be a clause that has been separated from its main sentence. For example:

Because more students want to live on campus.

This phrase whets the reader's appetite: What is going to happen because more students want to live on campus? Where is the rest of the sentence?

Because more students want to live on campus, GSU plans to build more dorms.

Fragments can often follow a complete sentence that they should be linked with:

More students want to study abroad. Since it gives them a global perspective on their studies.

The *since* clause belongs to the sentence it follows, and is clearer if directly connected:

More students want to study abroad, since it gives them a global perspective on their studies.

Subject/Verb Agreement

When writers discuss subjects agreeing with verbs, they mean that the subject of the sentence is followed by a verb that reflects the subject's singular or plural nature and its person (I, you, we, etc.). In most cases, English only changes the verb with the third person *he, she,* or *it.* So the same sentence with different subjects will have different verb forms:

*I **like** to cook a big breakfast before class.*

*She **likes** to cook a big breakfast before class.*

This is easy enough to do with a simple phrase; however, longer, more descriptive sentences often separate the subject from the verb, which can lead to a disagreement:

The author of the books we are using for the next several weeks are French.

The subject, *author*, is followed by some interesting detail that separates it from the verb. If the detail is removed, the sentence reads:

> *The author are French.*

The verb relating to *author* in its proper form should be *is*.

> *The author of the books we are using for the next several weeks is French.*

Subject/verb agreement is a problem that most spell-checking programs tend to overlook. The technological systems often mistakenly link the verb to whatever noun comes immediately before it, and in many cases, that noun is not the subject.

Possessives

In English, the most common way to show ownership or possession is to add an *'s* to a noun:

> *John's dorm room is on the ninth floor.*

The addition of the *'s* to *John* indicates that he is the owner of the dorm room on the ninth floor. In the case of nouns that are already plural, the *'s* is added the same way:

> *The men's basketball team has an away game this weekend.*

But the construction can be confusing if there are two or more people involved. For instance, what if the writer wants to indicate that two friends share a dorm room on the ninth floor? In this case, the apostrophe follows the final *s* in the word *friends*:

> *My friends' dorm room is on the ninth floor.*

By adding the apostrophe at the end of the plural word, the reader knows that there is more than one friend sharing the dorm room. The same sense is conveyed in this sentence:

> *The professor is concerned about the students' progress.*

Because the apostrophe follows the plural word *students*, the reader knows that the professor is worried about everyone in the class, not just one student in particular.

Tense Shifts

In academic writing such as research papers and essays, much of the information or action being relayed has already taken place, so the past tense is often the most appropriate choice. No matter what tense you select, you should use it consistently. This is particularly important within individual sentences. Shifting tenses between clauses in the same sentence can create reader confusion about what happened and when it happened. For example:

> *Someone pulled the fire alarm yesterday, so we get out of class without taking the quiz.*

The past tense *pulled* and the word *yesterday* are clear indications that the fire alarm happened in the past. Yet the second part of the sentence shifts into the present: *we get out of class*. Is the writer now referring to today's class? If all of this activity occurred yesterday, keep all the tenses in the past:

> *Someone pulled the fire alarm yesterday, so we got out of class without taking the quiz.*

Diction

Good diction, the ability to consistently choose the most accurate word for what you want to say, can make or break your writing; it can mean the difference between a reader actively engaging with and understanding your work, or walking away frustrated and bewildered. Many words sound alike but have distinctly different meanings. Others have different meanings if used with a contraction. Some of the most frequently confused word choices are:

Affect, effect: As a verb, *affect* means influence, and as a noun, *affect* means emotions or feelings. By contrast, *effect* is typically used as a noun and means results, but it can also be used as a verb to mean "bring about."

A part, apart: A *part* is a noun (*I need a part for the car*); *apart* is an adverb that means separated.

Cite, site, sight: Cite is to quote; *site* is a location (as on the Web); *sight* is something to see, as in a tourist destination.

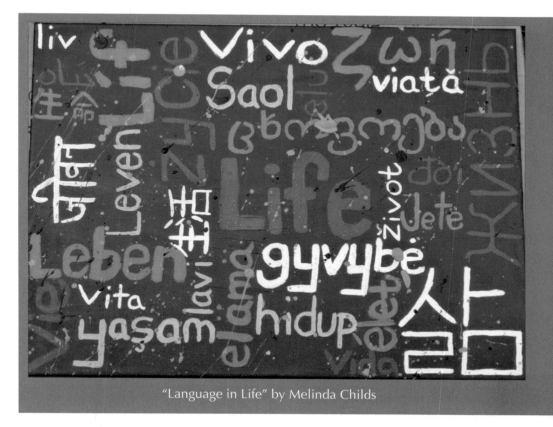

"Language in Life" by Melinda Childs

Compliment, complement: Compliment is a positive comment; a *complement* is a good match to something else (*That scarf is a perfect complement to her outfit*).

Its, it's: Its is the possessive form of it; *it's* is the contraction for "it is."

Lead, led: Lead is the present tense of the verb "to lead;" *led* is the past tense (*On St. Patrick's Day, he led the parade down Main Street*).

Lie, lay: Lie is to be recumbent (*I lie down for a nap after lunch*); *lay* takes an object (*I will lay the book on the table*).

Passed, past: Passed is a verb; *past* is an adjective or noun (*He has a shady past*).

Stationary, stationery: Stationary means to stand still; *stationery* means paper and envelopes.

Than, then: Than is a comparative word (*It is hotter today than yesterday*); *then* is an adverb of time (*Let's go to the gym, then we'll have lunch*).

Their, there, they're: There is the possessive for they; *there* indicates place; *there* is the contraction of "they are."

Your, you're: Your is the possessive of you; *you're* is the contraction of "you are."

Whether, weather: Whether indicates alternatives (*He is not sure whether he will pass or fail*); *weather* refers strictly to climate.

GETTING THE WORDS RIGHT

In an interview called "The Art of Fiction" with the *Paris Review* in 1956, Ernest Hemingway revealed his revision process:

Interviewer: How much rewriting do you do? *Hemingway:* It depends. I rewrote the ending of *Farewell to Arms*, the last page of it, *39 times* before I was satisfied. *Interviewer:* Was there some technical problem there? What was it that had stumped you? *Hemingway:* Getting the words right.

If a writer like Hemingway feels he must revise one page 39 times, what then does a student writer need to do? You may not have the opportunity to revise your writing 39 times, but remember the importance of taking revision seriously, and taking advantage of every opportunity to improve your writing.

In the same *Paris Review* article, drama critic, poet, and short story writer Dorothy Parker responded to a question about her writing process: "It takes me six months to do a story. I think it out and write it sentence by sentence—no first draft. I can't write five words but that I can change seven." Clearly, professional writers have individual processes and have practiced strategies that work for them. Also, they understand that writing is an art, and that the process of excellent writing is painstakingly slow. However, they also know that the payoff is a deep sense of satisfaction and accomplishment.

Engaging, effective writing, like all other skills, takes time and practice. We hope that from reading this chapter, you will take away these essential pieces of advice regarding the writing process:

1. Start work early on writing assignments, and pace yourself so that you may complete each portion in a timely and exemplary manner.

2. Read the assignment materials carefully, and communicate your questions and concerns to your instructor in class and during one-on-one conferences.

3. Initial drafts are messy. Try to generate as much material as possible and then shape it into something more polished. Think of someone making a pottery vase. He or she must have clay on the wheel in order to shape the vase. The first draft is the clay. When you write, you add "clay," remove clay and move clay around in order to make the vase. You must first have the clay. Enjoy both the "messy writer" phase and the "meticulous editor" phase.

4. Seek feedback on your work from peers and family members. Getting another set of eyes or ears to respond to your paper proves helpful in making sure that your ideas are clear and engaging.

5. Put forth effort into every phase of the process: prewriting, drafting, revising, editing, and proofreading.

6. Read your rhetoric text for help with content, organization, and style issues.

7. Refer to your grammar handbook for tips on correcting mistakes in grammar, usage, mechanics, documentation, and manuscript form. Make sure all sources are properly documented in the correct form (usually MLA).

8. Revise, revise, and revise some more. The great thing about writing is that it is never finished. You can always go back and make it better. Many instructors give the opportunity to revise work after it is graded. Take advantage of this opportunity to improve your writing.

Writing is a challenging and exciting journey. You see the results of our efforts immediately. Many people are available and willing to help you. Find strategies that work for you and use them. Enjoy the process!

APPENDIX OF STUDENT SAMPLE ESSAYS AND DISCUSSION QUESTIONS

Example One:

Blake Pilgrim
Ms. Olive
ENGL 1101
9 September 2012

A Trip to the Ballpark

I am known around my friends and family as somewhat of a sports-geek; I am sure right now you are imagining a typical jock who does not do much critical thinking and focuses on sports in only a literal sense. But my interest in sports is a little deeper than that. I look at sports in somewhat of a poetic way. To me, while it may sound silly to others, sports are beautiful. They require intricate strategies, and teach discipline and morals that could be used as metaphors that transcend to all facets of life. Sports are truly my passion in life. I dedicate a great deal of my time and brain power to carefully studying various stats, reading different articles on various media, analyzing strategies, breaking down the specifics of the game in pretty minute detail, and watching games of all types very closely. In researching sports, I take a scholarly approach. All of my love for sports can be traced back to the very first Braves game I attended with my dad in 1997. That day is the root of all my passion. It introduced me into my life-long love of sports, and really made me see what was so great about fandom.

From a very young age, I remember always watching sports on television with my dad, whether it was Georgia Tech football games, Falcons games, Braves games, or the Atlanta Hawks. I was about to turn four years old at the time, so I obviously did not have too much of an in-depth idea of what exactly was going on during the games. I had a basic understanding of how most of the games I watched worked, but probably could not explain them very well to anyone at the time. I enjoyed watching the games, but mainly I liked watching them with my dad. I used to be amazed at how loud he could yell and how he could possibly get so mad about a "bad" call or someone not doing their job very well. I was so young and fairly happy; I could never imagine getting that upset over anything. But I did not really look at my dad's anger with contempt; it was with more of a genuine curiosity. I wanted to understand how someone could be so passionate about something in which he was not directly involved.

My dad worked for Fayette Community Hospital (now called Piedmont Fayette Hospital) as a maintenance worker. He had previously been a construction worker and a carpenter, but wanted to work closer to home, so he got the position at the hospital where they often had ticket giveaways for the pro sports teams in the area. Piedmont Hospital had been dubbed the "Official Hospital" of most of the local franchises and, therefore, had a luxury suite at each of the local sports arenas. They would also give out tickets in other locations in the sports arenas, which in the case of the Braves game, usually ended up being behind home plate. Sure enough, with the buzz around the city for the Braves at the time, almost everybody who worked at Piedmont Hospital entered for a chance to win the tickets. In actuality, my dad did not end up winning the tickets himself. His co-worker won them, but she could not attend the game that day. She approached my dad knowing that he had a four year-old son at home who would be very happy to attend such an event, and she offered him the tickets. Of course he accepted them and thanked her. He came home and told me we were given tickets to the Braves game. I was elated! I would soon be on my way to see my first Atlanta Braves game.

It was in mid-April 1997, and the Braves were playing the Philadelphia Phillies. The game was scheduled for around one o'clock that day, so we left from our house at around eleven, so we could get there early for a good parking space and to take a look around the new stadium. We got into my dad's old burgundy three-seater 1990 Ford Ranger. There were tar stains on the inside of it from where my dad would go outside at night to listen to talk radio and smoke cigars, since my mom wouldn't allow him to do so inside. He popped in the Alan Jackson cassette tape I loved to listen to so much, and we were off.

I had never seen the city of Atlanta before. As we approached the stadium, I couldn't believe the size of the buildings. We were not even close to them, and they still seemed so huge! I lived in the suburbs and had only seen such things on television. We parked in a hotel parking lot just south of the stadium and began walking up to the main gate to enter the stadium. I could not believe how many people I saw there outside of the stadium, walking to the same place we were. There was a vendor's stand on our way there, and as any curious kid would, I stopped to look at the various shirts, jerseys, hats, baseball cards, and other gear they sold. I did not actually own any Braves paraphernalia at the time, so my dad bought me a Braves hat. I still have the tiny adjustable cap, with its trademarked italicized white "A" on it, and its red bill and navy top, sitting in my room to this day. That day I proudly put my cap on, and we continued making our way to our seats along with thousands of other fans.

I had thought there were a lot of people outside, but that paled in comparison to the number of people who were actually in the stadium. I had never seen so many people in one spot in my entire life. Given the Braves' recent success, and the fact that the Braves were playing their first season in their brand new stadium, Turner Field, the atmosphere was electric. Our seats were directly behind home plate, about twenty rows up or so. We sat next to one of my dad's co-workers. I don't remember her name, but I do remember she was a larger woman with an even larger laugh. I was shy at first, but she was nice, and I ended up talking her ear off during the game. Once the game got underway, I was taken back. The real-time action and speed of the game blew my mind. At one point, a foul ball was hit near us, and someone caught it using his hat. I asked my dad if he was going to give it back, and he told me the man got to keep it. I could not believe it! Instantly I had an intense desire to catch my own foul ball. In addition to the occasional foul ball, there were cotton candy vendors walking around, people yelling everywhere, and "jumbotron" with players' pictures on it. It was a lot for me to take in. I was simply amazed.

The game was pretty monotonous outside of the Phillies' early scoring, until a late-rallying moment really caught my attention. Probably around the seventh inning or so (although I cannot exactly remember), the Braves began mounting a comeback. They loaded the bases up, and Brian Jordan, the Braves' right fielder in the prime of his career, headed to bat. The Phillies' manager headed to the mound to make a pitching change and, when that happened, the crowd erupted with the famous "Tomahawk Chop." The "chop" is a rallying cry of sorts that Braves fans picked up in the early nineties from Florida State University fans. It basically involves people chopping their hand up and down at the elbow while reciting a chant of "oh's" at different tones.

"ReEdit." by Patrick Duffy.

It may sound dumb to some people, but I marveled at the crowd doing the chop in unison, with that lovely chant bellowing into my ears. Brian Jordan would go on to hit a home run, and the crowd would go bonkers. Just in that moment, I had fallen in love with the Braves.

After that game, I began trying to watch as many sporting events with my dad as possible, but now I took an interest in the game itself, not just spending time with my dad. I would always ask to be signed up to play baseball, although I was not old enough yet. Sports also would begin to show through in other parts of my life. In art class, whenever we would draw pictures, I would work on perfecting drawing the Braves' logo, or a picture of a Falcons game, or whoever was my favorite athlete at the time. From that moment, a lifetime of fandom sprung. I loved the feeling of being a part of something bigger than myself, of being a part of almost a "brotherhood" of sorts with fellow Atlanta sports fans. This only grew stronger as I got older and could better understand all the happenings with the teams I followed. In my mind, sports were a consistency in my life. While you may lose contact with friends and acquaintances throughout your life, you could never lose contact with your favorite team. All of that started with one trip to a Braves game with my dad, and has not ended since.

Example Two:

Deranda B.
Danielle Weber
English 1102
9 April 2012

Thrifting Makes Cents

Next week Janice is throwing a huge party, but Erica and her friend, Ashley, have no idea as to what they are going to wear. Even with a closet and two dressers full of clothes, the two girls feel the urge to buy something new for the event. While most American teenagers would seize this opportunity to visit the mall, Erica and Ashley have a different plan in mind. They are going "thrifting," a term used when people go to thrift stores like Goodwill and Value Village to find items (usually clothes) at a significantly cheaper price than at a department store. Most people love to go to retailers like Forever 21 and H&M to fill their closets; however, thrifting is more cost effective, can be more fun, is environmentally friendly, and helps the surrounding community.

Thrifting saves a remarkable amount of money. According to Danielle Vermeer, the average American woman spends between 1,000 and 2,000 dollars every year on clothes, and she will only wear about 25 percent of what is in her closet. That's less than half of her belongings. Thrifting helps consumers to avoid wasting money on clothing and apparel. Many people would love to have ten items in their hand and only pay 20 dollars for it. A thirty-dollar shirt at the mall costs just four dollars at a thrift store. That is an 18-dollar difference! Thrifting is extremely beneficial for fashionably-inclined college students. It helps them satisfy their wants, while at the same time not breaking their pockets. In 2011 *KomoNews* published a report about Beautiful Existence (her real name) from Seattle, who saved more than 13,000 dollars by strictly shopping at Goodwill (a well-known thrift store) for an entire year (Whitaker). Beautiful shopped for her entire family and was able to provide them with gently-used, but fashionable items. She even bought her husband a one hundred-dollar watch for his birthday, which is a significantly reduced price than the original three hundred-dollar tag. Thrift stores give the shopper a way to stretch her dollar.

Aside from saving money, thrifting also makes a person unique. Department store racks are filled with the same items in different sizes. Yet, a thrift store contains numerous pieces of clothing that no one else owns. Some of these items are "retro" or from boutique shops or stores in different states or countries. No one wants to look like a clone; so thrifting is a good way to stand out. Looking for a pair of pants from the 90's or something that looks vintage or retro-chic? There is no better place to go than the thrift store. Searching through the racks and boxes at a discount store can be fun, because the clothes have character – they tell their own story. Each article of clothing being donated or sold to a discount store has a reason for being discarded. Maybe something reminded a woman of a bad break up and she tossed it. Maybe a young professional wore that lime-green pant suit on her first job interview. Who knows? The possibilities are endless. Well-known fashion blogger and vintage thrifti-er Elissa Stern says "A thrift store is not just rows of cast off clothing, it's a library of endless stories." When someone shops at a thrift store he or she takes on the narrative of another person and continues it. The fact that thrift stores do not follow the latest trends, and a variety of people give their belongings to them, makes them very fun and diverse places to shop, no matter what your style.

While you are having fun shopping, thrifting is also a fantastic way to help the environment. Each time a person goes to the thrift store to purchase an already-used item she is saving our planet. It takes approximately 1,800 gallons of water to grow enough cotton to produce a single pair of blue jeans, and about 400 gallons for a plain cotton t-shirt (Merchant). That is roughly 2,200 gallons of water to make one outfit. By simply going to the local thrift store and purchasing gently-used clothes, shoppers aid in saving the planet by not putting a huge strain on water usage. Similarly, some people tend to kill animals in order to make nice leather boots and jackets. Instead of going to the mall to purchase a new leather jacket, an environmentally conscious shopper can purchase a similar jacket at a thrift store, which does not require the death of another animal. This practice benefits the environment because more animals get to keep their lives. With that being said, animals are allowed to stay in their natural environment, which aids in keeping a balance in the food chain. If buying items at lower prices is not enough to convince shoppers to thrift, then maybe being a good environmentalist will.

Thrifting does not only help the environment, it can help other people, too. Items donated to thrift stores help those who are economically challenged. All of the items in the store are usually donated to shelters and completely free to those in need. The clothes are donated ones that did not sell in a certain time frame. When shelters and thrift stores collaborate, it puts clothes on the backs of the homeless. Many people who are less fortunate than others are trying to get back on their feet. If a homeless man had access to a collared shirt and a pair of slacks, it could possibly change his life. An even better example would be the Salvation Army. They are not only the people who ring bells during Christmas time, but they are also working to make America a better nation year-round. The Salvation Army has been accepting donations and selling products at extremely low prices since 1881 (The Salvation Army). A person could go anywhere to shop. Yet, I believe it is better to shop at a thrift store because a portion of the proceeds go to help others in their time of need.

On the other hand, there are people who oppose thrift stores and avoid them like the plague. First and foremost, some people find it disgusting or unsanitary to buy used goods. The staff members at Goodwill and other bargain places are pretty good about cleaning up the products before they put them out for sale. They deal with so many items from a great number of people from many different places that it would be completely unsanitary for them not to. There are no dirty or foul-smelling clothes on a racks at thrift stores; but, to be on the safe side, a customer should also wash the things they buy before using them. This rule applies to new store-bought clothes as well. There are many products like bleach, soap and water, Oxyclean, and liquid detergent that will kill germs and have clothes and everything else looking as good as new.

Another major issue most people have with shopping in thrift stores is how unorganized it is. While these types of places do not have clothing sizes in order, and may have books next to kitchen utensils, they are still fairly organized by an item's usage. The thrift stores do in fact separate the clothes by pants, shirts, dresses, shoes, and so on. The employees work hard to try and keep things that coincide with each other like pillows and mattresses together. The fact that these establishments are so diverse and have a unique inventory makes it more difficult for them to organize everything perfectly—as one would see inside a store in the mall. Yes, thrifting is time consuming but it can be enjoyable – especially if treating it as a game or a challenge. While it may take more time to dig through some boxes, the fun is in what can be found there.

Ultimately, going thrifting with Erica and Ashley before running to the mall is the best decision. The majority of the girls who attend the party have gone to the same stores. They have bought the same party outfit and each of them feels as if they will be "that girl" for the night. But Erica and Ashley did not take the common route to the mall. They were the ones who stood out and command the attention. While thrifting may seem like a bad idea to people who are opposed to used goods or spending an increased amount of time shopping, the benefits outweigh the negatives. Thrifting provides unique items; it helps the environment and the less fortunate, and it saves consumers money. It is a reward within itself. In today's economy thrifting makes great cents.

Works Cited

Merchant, Brian. "How Many Gallons of Water Does it Take to Make..." *Tree Hugger.* Tree Hugger, 29 June 2011. Web. 7 Apr. 2012.

Stern, Elissa L. *Thrifting 101: A Beginner's Guide to Thrifting and Vintage.* England: Dress with Courage, n.d. 7-11. Print.

The Salvation Army. The Salvation Army, n.d. Web. 9 Apr. 2012.

Vermeer, Danielle. "Save Thousands of Dollars Each Year with These Thrift Store Strategies." *The Crazy Coupon Lady.* KCL, 18 Mar. 2012. Web. 8 Apr. 2012.

Whitaker, Denise. "Local mom saves thousands by shopping at nonprofits." *KomoNews.com* 26 Dec. 2011 *[Seattle].* Web. 8 Apr. 2012.

For Discussion

In whole class discussion or in small groups, answer the following questions about each sample essay:

1. What is the thesis or main idea? If there is an explicit thesis statement, indicate where it is in the essay. If the thesis statement is implied, explain what you believe the main idea or claim to be. Does the writer maintain this focus?

2. Does the writer engage the audience with an interesting "hook" in the introduction?

3. How does the writer employ an appropriate organizational structure for the argument within the essay? Does each paragraph focus on a single topic, or more than one? Does the paper flow with good transitioning?

4. Does the writer appeal to ethos, pathos, or logos? If so, comment on what you found interesting or engaging about his or her use of these appeals. If not, offer a few suggestions as to where and how the writer might revise to strengthen these elements.

5. How does the writer conclude the essay? Does the writer do more than merely summarize the main points of the essay? What additional insight does the writer add at the end? If none has been added, what insight do you feel could be added to make the conclusion stronger?

6. What do you believe to be the strengths and weaknesses of this essay?

Two

Analysis

Analytical writing requires more than simply preparing a summary. Each discipline and college major requires students to think critically and make analytical arguments that consider the deeper significance of an idea, a text, an event, or a process. This chapter addresses how to perform effective analysis and convey those ideas.

SUMMARY VERSUS ANALYSIS

Generally, students in English composition classes write synopses of materials and present this information as a paper or essay. Often the approach to writing a summary is to include elements commonly referred to as the "6 Ws," answering the questions who, what, when, where, why, and how. The writer, relying upon his or her own words, condenses and offers an explanation of the essential elements of the material. A condensed version that reports what the author presented—rather than the student's interpretation—is called a **summary**.

As students become more adept at summarizing texts, their instructors will often encourage them to begin analyzing what they read. In an analysis, students are asked to go beyond simply summarizing and instead offer critical interpretations of various modes of expression. An analytical thinker will read a text not only to understand what it says but also to see how it works. The resulting analysis will then offer an interpretation or judgment of the text that the author supports with evidence.

Text refers to the wide variety of materials students are called upon to analyze in their college careers. In the humanities, the term **text** often refers to poems, short stories, academic journal articles, novels as well as speeches, journalism pieces, essays, comics, photographs, or movies. In composition courses, students will likely analyze written documents, images, films, or physical objects. The analysis may also include evaluation of an important event in the student's life or particular aspects of society and culture.

"Untitled" by Charles Clark

In other disciplines, the materials for analysis may include these same items but could also extend to other media, artifacts, or materials. For example, a geology student might analyze the features of Stone Mountain to establish the conditions of its formation. A marketing student might evaluate a recent Coca-Cola advertisement, engaging in analysis to determine the ad's effectiveness. A music student might examine the structure of Beethoven's "Moonlight Sonata" to better understand its emotional power. An exercise science student might gather information about an individual's diet and lifestyle choices in order to develop a sustainable regimen for improved health. All of these critical thinking exercises require more than simply summarizing the information gathered or observed. Analysis is a tool for uncovering deeper meaning.

To further illustrate differences between summary and analysis, consider the practice of interpreting dreams in psychoanalysis. One common dream centers on the dreamer showing up to work, school, or some other public place completely naked. In all likelihood, everyone reading this book has had the naked dream or one very much like it. Summarizing this dream is easy: "I was running down the hall of Aderhold because I was late for an exam, and when I burst into the classroom everybody turned to me and started laughing. When I looked down, I realized that I wasn't wearing any clothes. . . ." This summary encapsulates the events of the dream; here we have what actually happens in the dream, the plot of the little movie that the dreamer watches while asleep.

As psychoanalysis argues, this dream is about something else. The scenario is a classic example of an anxiety dream where the embarrassing act of showing up to class naked is really the unconscious mind's attempt to process a worry about something else (like that exam). The dreamer's fear about taking the exam constitutes the deeper or latent meaning of the dream. In a written format, the summary would describe the events in the dream, but the analysis would point to the elements that reveal the *meaning*.

COMPONENTS OF ANALYSIS

All analysis involves **claims**, **criteria**, and **evidence**. A claim asserts a particular viewpoint or interpretation, while criteria are the standards the student uses to judge the text. Evidence, as one can probably guess, provides support for the claim. Below are simple examples of how a claim, criteria, and evidence work together for effective analysis:

Claim: The Iron Man movies affirm the longevity and popularity of comic book heroes in twenty-first century culture.

Criteria: This claim considers the sales of Iron Man comic books, movie tickets, and action figures.

Evidence: Iron Man, through comic book, movie ticket, and action figures sales showed an increase in sales in the twenty-first century as the films were released.

Analysis always involves criteria. Criteria can be described as either **subjective** or **objective**. Subjective criteria include personal preferences, impressions, and feelings that stem from a person's unique history or experiences. As a result, subjective criteria can vary from one individual to another. Think about the language friends might use in arguing for one movie interpretation or another: "I think superhero movies are dumb. . . . I love that French actor, whatshisname. . . . Reading subtitles is boring." Each of these statements employs subjective criteria, signaled by the use of the first person "I-voice," emotionally charge verbs, or adjectives such as "dumb," "love," and "boring."

In contrast, objective analysis moves from the perspective of one person or a small group to focusing on the inclusion of claims and evidence that are broadly accepted. Objective analysis largely works to remove information that might be considered biased. As a result, objective criteria remains the same regardless of the individual who employs it. Consider how friends might objectively evaluate a movie: "While I think superhero movies are dumb, the movie won four Oscars, including best picture and best director." In this same vein, discussions about the film's plot, the names of characters, and setting are independently verifiable facts, and therefore do not change based upon the individual.

While personal preferences have value in the composition classroom, academic writing challenges us as writers to move to more objective, analytical thinking, and writing. A **claim**, also known as the writer's primary assertion or thesis statement, is strongest when supported by **evidence** based upon objective criteria—criteria that is supported by research or confirmed data. Determining whether statements are subjective or objective calls upon the writer to consider the standards by which materials are evaluated. If the statement can change based upon the individual who makes it, it is likely a subjective statement. For example, "Georgia State University's downtown location makes it a unique place to go to college." The insertion of "unique" without supporting evidence or facts makes it a subjective statement because the definition of what makes something unique will vary from person to person. In contrast, a statement such as "Georgia State University's almost 32,000 students make it one of the largest urban universities in the South" is an objective statement because size is something that can be independently confirmed by measurement. To strengthen this objective statement further, a student could include statistics that compare and contrast Georgia State University to other southern universities. If the statistics show that GSU indeed has more students and/or land in an urban area, this would be objective information that could support a subjective statement regarding GSU's uniqueness. In other words, one could cite the size of the campus as one of the things that makes GSU a unique place to attend college.

"GSU" by James Supreme

ANALYTICAL WRITING IN COMPOSITION COURSES

Many writing assignments in first-year composition courses ask students to produce essays that rely primarily on analysis. These essays may take the form of a rhetorical, textual, or visual analysis. While the specifics of the assignment will vary, the essay will almost certainly require the following elements:

- a brief summary of the text providing the information that readers need to understand your analysis
- a clear and arguable claim
- reasonable support for the claim with pertinent details from the text or backing from reputable sources

Depending on the instructor or the focus of the particular composition course, the "text" you examine could be any number of things:

- an advertisement
- a static image, like a photograph or painting
- a political speech
- a persuasive essay
- a piece of imaginative writing (poem or short story)
- a movie or documentary
- a public or private place
- an event where people come together for a common purpose
- a process, or the steps one takes to complete a certain task or make a certain impression in others
- a phenomenon and its causes
- a culture or group of people (ethnography)
  *For further discussion, see *Chapter 6: Writing through Culture*

In order to understand how your text works and creates meaning, you will want to closely examine its individual parts and ask questions of the text. The answers to these questions can provide great fodder for your essay:

- What is the text's rhetorical situation?
- Are there any elements highlighted or emphasized by the author?
- Does the author noticeably omit important information?
- Does the author make use of any rhetorical appeals? (logos, pathos, ethos)
- Does the text contain repetitive elements such as words, phrases, or images that are present throughout?
- Does the text use color, sound, or music?
- Does the author use any symbolic language or imagery?
- How is the text structured or organized? Is there a noticeable pattern at work in the text?
- What sources does the author use? Are they reliable? Are they biased?
- How is the text composed? Are the elements placed in the foreground, background, top, bottom, left, right, or center of an image/film/screen/document?

After you ask questions like these, you will want to follow up with perhaps the most important ones: So what? What does any of this mean? For instance, if you notice that an artist only uses red paint in the piece you are analyzing, the next questions to ask might include: Well, what does that mean? What does the red paint represent? Why did the artist select red paint? Here you make your analytical leap to say, "The artist exclusively

"March 11" by Patrick Duffy

uses red in this painting in order to communicate her rage against the art establishment." The question about color in the painting, then, led to an analytical claim—the heart of a written analysis.

CRITICAL COMPONENTS OF A TEXTUAL ANALYSIS

Summary

A textual analysis contains some summary because the audience may not be familiar with the text an author is analyzing. The amount of summary in an analytical essay will vary depending on the familiarity of the text. If a student were writing an essay on Martin Luther King Jr.'s "I Have a Dream" speech, for example, the writer would not need to give very much information about the speech because it is such a familiar text for most student readers. The lyrics from an obscure punk album, on the other hand, may need more explanation depending upon the audience. While a textual analysis should include some summary, the majority of the essay should be analysis.

Unique Interpretation

A textual analysis should present an arguable interpretation of the text that the author typically introduces in a thesis statement. In an analysis of a short story, for example, an author might argue that the story's first-person narration forces readers to see events from a narrow perspective and raises questions about the protagonist's reliability. Or, in an analytical paper on a newspaper op-ed piece, a student might argue that the writer uses hyperbolic or exaggerated language in order to highlight the absurdity of a particular political stance.

Support

No matter the unique interpretation put forward in a textual analysis, the writer must offer support for his or her debatable claim. Support for the thesis statement might come from the text itself or it may come from outside sources. In the example of the op-ed piece given above, the student would likely include a couple of specific examples where the writer uses hyperbolic language and then explains how these instances work to prove that the op-ed satirizes a political platform.

The following excerpt from a textual analysis illustrates how a writer supports an analytical claim based on a non-fiction essay.

Summary:

Dave Barry vividly describes the execution of a prisoner in an electric chair while also telling his readers about the man's crime.

Claim:

In his essay, "Chronicle of an American Execution," Dave Barry compares a prisoner on death row to a "young child" in order to emphasize the man's helplessness and the peculiar irony of capital punishment.

Support:

Barry introduces readers to a man about to be electrocuted by the state of Tennessee: "He looks almost like a young child buckled into a car seat." The comparison of this inmate to a child underscores the man's lack of control. He does not buckle himself, but is "buckled." Like a child in the back seat of a car, this prisoner is along for the ride--helpless, at this point, to turn back or change course.

Barry's illustration also makes clear that capital punishment is a deeply ironic tool of justice. The prisoner, ten years earlier, shot and killed his four children. Now, this man sits like a child, waiting to be killed himself. Barry does not declare this man innocent in comparing him to a child, but he does show his readers what looming death makes of all people. Death makes them helpless like children.

CRITICAL COMPONENTS OF A VISUAL ANALYSIS

Summary

An effective visual analysis nearly always contains some summary at or near the beginning. The content of this summary depends on whether the analysis deals with a single still image, a series of still images, or a series of moving images. In the case of a still image like a photograph, a painting, or a drawing, this summary will likely begin by identifying the image's medium (e.g. digital photograph, oil painting, pencil drawing) as well as what the image depicts. The summary will then move on to describe the image's basic composition in terms of color and the arrangement of the image's component parts. For instance, in the case of Leonardo da Vinci's iconic *Mona Lisa* painting, a student analyzing the image might begin his or her summary by stating that the portrait is an oil painting depicting a young woman with a very faint smile on her face. The student might then go on to mention that the painting employs a subdued color scheme with a lot of blacks and browns, and that the painting's subject, the young woman, appears in the foreground of the painting with a rocky landscape and a lake in the background.

VISUAL ANALYSIS: Summary

Consider the following photo, which was taken by Joshua Yu, a student at Georgia State University. What information is crucial to constructing a **summary** analysis? You may also want to consider the following: Joshua Yu is a student at GSU. The photo was taken in downtown Atlanta during the International Flag Parade. Joshua submitted the photo as part of a contest for the *Guide to First Year Writing,* 2nd edition.

"International Flag Parade 1" by Joshua Yu

In the case of a series of images as in a comic, or a collection of moving images like a film, the summary will focus more on the narrative told through the series of images. It is not necessary to summarize every single action in the narrative when analyzing a series of images. Instead, the summary should provide a sense of the overall story being told through images. The subsequent supporting paragraphs of the analysis might bring up more in-depth aspects of the plot in order to make specific points about the images being analyzed. However, these plot elements should be chosen very selectively based on the argument the writer wishes to make about the series of images. The initial summary simply ensures that when the writer brings up a more in-depth aspect of the plot later on, the reader will not become confused as to how this aspect relates to the overall story told through the series of images.

As with a textual analysis, the amount of summary included in a visual analysis will depend on the audience's familiarity with the selected image(s). An analysis of the *Mona Lisa*, for instance, would probably require less summary than, say, a painting by a GSU art student. The *Mona Lisa* is a very familiar image to most people, while the newly completed painting by the GSU art student is possibly known only to a small community.

Unique Interpretation

As with a textual analysis, a visual analysis should offer a unique, arguable interpretation of the materials under review. So what qualifies as a unique, arguable interpretation of an image or series of images? Suppose a student wrote a visual analysis with the following thesis statement: "The *Mona Lisa* is a famous Italian painting that has captivated millions since Leonardo da Vinci painted it in the sixteenth century." An assertion of this nature does not constitute visual analysis that shows a unique, arguable interpretation of the *Mona Lisa*. In fact, it would not be providing an interpretation at all: this statement is simply an observation and stating of a historical fact. Suppose the same student then revised her visual analysis to argue about specific qualities of the painting that account for its ability to captivate viewers such as "The eyes in the painting are the key to its unique power as they appear to follow viewers as they move. The deep brown of the irises, settled against the whites of the eyes show Mona Lisa's intense and deep focus on what is in front of her." Such an analysis presents a unique, arguable interpretation of the painting.

Support

First and foremost, a unique interpretation of an image's meaning or influence requires support based on references to specific elements of the image. For instance, a writer might discuss the significance of the colors a painter used or the impact of a photographer's decision to take a photograph from a particular angle or under certain lighting conditions. An argument, however, about an image's meaning or effects can also refer to outside sources. For example, a writer might support her own claim by referencing what an art scholar has said about the image being analyzed.

The following excerpt from a visual analysis will help illustrate how a writer supports an analytical claim based on a single image.

Summary:

Nadia Deljou's black-and-white photograph *Sin Limitaciones* depicts a scene from an ordinary city street. A thick iron chain runs diagonally through the foreground of the photograph. Beyond the chain, in the background, the viewer can see a dirty brick walkway and a concrete wall with "THINK!" spraypainted across it.

Claim:

Through her photograph, Nadia Deljou urges viewers to use critical thinking and analysis as a means to free their minds from the figurative chains binding them and live a life "*sin limitaciones* [without limitations]."

"Sin Limitaciones" by Nadia Deljou

Support:

The thick iron chain running diagonally through the foreground represents the limitations that Deljou wishes the viewers to overcome in their lives. Chains have long symbolized slavery and a lack of freedom. By placing the chain in hard focus in the foreground, Deljou presents the chain as a visual metaphor for the prejudices and received ideas that enslave people's minds. The chain tries to control the way that the viewer sees, interprets, and thinks about the photograph by being the most prominent and defined object in view. Indeed, a viewer who does not look and think closely about the photograph may not even really notice anything beside the chain.

The spraypainted word "THINK!" on the concrete wall in the background of the photograph indicates how viewers can free themselves from the tyranny of the chain. The chain's dominance in the photograph has forced the word to appear slightly out-of-focus. Visually, the blurriness of "THINK!" reproduces the effect that prejudices and received ideas tend to have upon thinking. When they dominate a person's thoughts, such mental restraints prevent individuals from thinking clearly and making good decisions. Deljou's photograph suggests that if viewers were to think more critically and analytically about the world around them, the chain would exercise less control over them, thereby enabling viewers to move freely, "without limitations."

Visual Analysis: Try These Two On Your Own

Now you know the difference between summary and analysis. Consider the photos below and outline the interpretations needed to create a **summary** for each of them. Once you have a summary of the photo, work to create a **claim** and then provide the support needed for the claim. Discuss the difference between your summary and your analysis.

"Holi—Festival of Colors 1" by Joshua Yu

"Come to Learn; Go to Serve" by Nadia Deljou

Analysis in Writing: A Sample Student Essay

Now that you have tried summary and analysis on your own, take a look at Jocelyn Lopez's essay "My Frappuccino: A Rhetorical Analysis of a Caffein-ated Commercial" as an example of a successful student model of analysis.

Introduction:

In the summer of 2011, television viewers around the nation tuned in to witness America's most popular coffee shop franchise, Starbucks, release its "however-you-want-it" Frappuccino blended beverage commercial. The purpose of the TV commercial is to sell Starbucks' unique product: a blended iced beverage that one can customize with various kinds of milk, toppings, and flavors. The ad was aired in May of 2011, a time when the weather is warm in many parts of the United States, therefore making an iced beverage a refreshing choice for potential customers. Un-like any other Starbucks' commercial, this one in particular incorporates many unique rhetorical elements packed in a fast-paced, thirty-second TV commercial. From the young, animated actors to each detailed ingredient used to make the Frappuccino, this commercial is packed with spontaneity and flavor within each second. Starbucks' 2011 summer commercial successfully utilizes its layout, highlighted elements and symbolism to advertise the "however-you-want-it" Frappuccino blended beverage and attract customers to the company and to its products.

1. What does the author need to know about the commercial? What does the author need to assume the audience knows?
2. How does Jocelyn contextualize the advertisement? In other words, how does she make sure the audience has all the information needed to un-derstand her analysis?
3. Can you find Jocelyn's analysis of the commercial in a centralized (the-sis) statement?

Concrete Details:

Apart from the commercial's layout, Starbucks has incorporated many visual elements to emphasize the advertised beverage. The commercial clearly displays these visual elements. When the commercial begins, a large plastic Starbucks cup is suddenly set heavily onto the table, making a loud crashing sound and grabbing the viewer's attention. Starbucks' newest green logo on the cup stands out among the white background, introducing the advertised brand. Other elements highlighted throughout the commercial include the ingredients used to make the beverage: coffee beans, coconuts, caramel, strawberries, chocolate, ice, milk, etc. These ingredients are the focus of the advertisement and are shown whirring in a blender, since the beverage is in fact a "blended" drink. The coffee beans are shown swirling in a clockwise direction as though they are being blended. The clockwise direction could symbolize the progression the Starbuck's company has made over the years as well as the company's success with their new drinks. An actor's hand squeezes the juice of strawberries over a sea of strawberries, illustrating how fresh fruits blend in the process. Also, a block of ice is smashed with a hammer, showing the crushed iced used for iced beverages. The advertisers purposely enhance these elements to make the ingredients stand out in a unique way compared to other commercials that simply show the finished product. Ultimately, these shots of the individual ingredients make the product seem even more appetizing for potential customers.

1. How does Jocelyn organize her description of the commercial? Is her organization effective, or do you have suggestions for improving her delivery

2. Is this paragraph mostly *summarizing* or *analyzing*?

Description and Analysis:

Furthermore, the use of symbolism in the Starbucks commercial reveals embedded meanings behind some of the images shown. For one, a barista holds a small trophy in the air during the middle of the commercial, symbolizing the success of the Starbucks brand and its products, attracting those who would like good-quality beverages. The toy dog and the piñata symbolize youth and innocence. These objects tie in with the feeling one might get when he or she tries this beverage, the feeling of being young again and having the "kid-in you" shine through, despite drinking a "grown-up" beverage such as coffee. Other parts of the commercial support this "child-like" theme, such as when a raucous customer throws a pie gets at a young man's face, when the female actor jumps up in joy on what might be a trampoline, and when the young man squirts a can of whip cream into his mouth. The actors' relative youth represents another form of symbolism. The actors are all young men and woman, ranging from teenagers to those in their early twenties, which clearly demonstrates the intended audience for this commercial. The actors also represent different nationalities and people of all races to Starbucks.

1. How is this paragraph and its intent different from the one directly above it?

2. What claims does this paragraph allow Jocelyn to make? Try to sum up her claims in one sentence.

Claim:

Overall, Starbucks successfully advertised its Frappuccino blended beverage during the summer of 2011. Its layout - a fast-paced, thirty-second commercial packed with much detail- keeps its audiences' attention and interest. The use of visually-appealing, aural, and verbal components also highlights particular images used. Furthermore, words and color equally play important roles in the commercial, emphasizing the ingredients the company uses when making the beverage. Finally, symbolism brings out the deeper meaning in the images used in order to attract the viewers to Starbucks and its products. As a whole, the components of the commercial did not only make viewers aware of the Starbuck's brand and the Frappuccino beverage, but also created an advertisement that was both convincing and enjoyable to watch.

The conclusion to Jocelyn's essay answers the following question: what response does the advertiser hope to achieve from his audience? Since Jocelyn believes the commercial achieves the feeling it sets out to obtain from its target audience, she supports this claim with the details she provides throughout the paper.

Analyzing Georgia State University's First-Year Book: *Beyond Katrina: a Meditation on the Mississippi Gulf Coast* by Natasha Trethewey

As first-year students, you were even given a copy of *Beyond Katrina: A Meditation on the Mississippi Gulf Coast* by Natasha Trethewey, Poet Laureate of the United States, 2012–2013. As part of the Georgia State University's First-Year Book Program, all incoming students read this text and were invited to listen to the author speak during orientation. Below are some exercises you can use to hone your summary and analysis skills. These exercises blend various textual mediums (see discussion of **text** earlier in this chapter). Additionally, the varying forms of textual summary and analysis provide practice for more advanced writing—writing

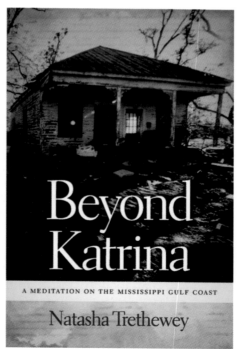

www.npr.org.

that requires analysis and evidence as a way to support an argument (see *Chapter Three: Analysis to Argument*).

Exercise One: *Natasha Trethewey in Her Own Words*

View the link posted to the *Guide to First Year Writing* companion website of Natasha's discussion of *Beyond Katrina* at GSU's Freshman Orientation. Take some time to summarize the main points she makes in her talk.

1.   Treat the Trethewey discussion as a piece of text. What summary can you provide of her talk? How does this summary allow you to develop claims for an analysis of the talk and its connection to the book?

2.   What are elements you gleaned from the talk that you missed when reading the book for the first time? How do these "new" elements affect your analysis of the book as a whole?

3.   How does hearing the author (either in person or through the video provided) change your interaction with the text?

Exercise Two: *What does O'Connor have to do with Katrina?*

Trethewey includes a quote from Fannery O'Conner's first novel *Wise Blood* as a forward to her book:

"Where you came from is gone. Where you thought you were going to never was there. And where you are is no good unless you can get away from it."

1.   What do these lines *mean* to you? Can you summarize this meaning?

2.   Take your summarization and develop a claim. For instance, do the lines *mean* places, though geographically "real" are fictions constructed by those who visit or live in them? And, if they are fictions, can they be reconstructed through the process of textualizing them (writing a book about them)?

3.   Now consider the claim you have made about the O'Connor quote and how it applies to the Trethewey text. Use parts of *Beyond Katrina* to support your claim.

Exercise Three: *Recovering the Landmass between Louisiana and Alabama*

One of the purposes of *Beyond Katrina* is to document and recover the loss of Mississippian identity post-Katrina.

1.   Do a Google search of "Landmass between New Orleans and Mobile." What types of *texts* do you find? You should find news articles, blogs, visuals, academic responses to the categorization of Mississippi as a mere "Landmass." Summarize the points made by these texts.

2. Analyze the influence these voices have in the process of recovering Mississippian identity.

Exercise Four: *Poems and Images*

Trethewey includes a table of contents of images published in *Beyond Katrina*. Additionally, the novel has several poems that are meant to provide commentary on the prose.

1. Look at the images in the text as a series of images. Summarize the effect these images have on the notions of identity, recovery, and meditation in the book.

2. Choose one of the poems published in the text. Analyze how this poem creates a textual dialogue between the intent of the prose and what you see as the "meaning" of the poem.

Conclusion

These examples give a sense for what successful analyses do: they go beyond the surface and expose a deeper meaning in a text. Analysis is more than summary—it prompts both the writer and the reader to consider the subject matter in unique ways that can prompt different interpretations and discussion. You may find you enjoy the freedom and challenges provided by analytical writing because it presents opportunities for you to express your views about culture, art, or other topics in the world around you. Analytical thinking and writing takes practice, so do not be discouraged if you have trouble writing this way at the start. Keep pushing yourself to ask questions and offer interpretations of the texts you encounter. Just remember to develop strong claims, identify criteria for analysis, and include evidence that supports your assertions.

Three

Analysis to Argument

In *Chapter Two: Analysis,* you learned several ways to summarize and then analyze the materials you encounter—you have techniques, now, to turn your ideas into written expression. Analysis is a building block to argumentation: summary → analysis → argument.

So, what is argument? Argument doesn't mean fighting. In fact, those who resort to yelling and flailing their arms with angry expressions on their faces often *lose* the argument, from an intellectual point of view. Argument is a mode of communication in which the speaker (or writer) appeals to his/her audience in order to convince them to see things from the speaker's point of view. Argument isn't about "winning." It's about being understood and having your point of view validated (even if others disagree). Academic argument guides the audience from one point to the next in a logical and ethical way; it starts with *claims* and *reasons* and is backed by *example* and *evidence*. The goal of academic argument, then, becomes to encourage your audience to think differently, to take action, or to feel safe to contribute ideas to the conversation. The argument, therefore, fosters dialogue between two people or among groups of people. You can imagine, then, how raised voices, claims lacking logical structure or evidentiary support, and a disregard for the audience pose a detriment to the goals of academic argument.

THE RHETORICAL SITUATION

You may hear your composition instructor use the word "rhetoric" when discussing ways to make your writing more powerful. Though most of us encounter the term *rhetoric* during political campaign seasons, the term is **not** a synonym for propaganda. When you use rhetoric ethically, you employ strategies for making your writing more focused, direct, and persuasive. Plato defined rhetoric as "the art of winning the soul by discourse." Aristotle, another Greek philosopher, viewed rhetoric as the "faculty of discovering in any particular case all of the available means of persuasion." Whether the aim is to win over the soul through the art of persuasion, or to simply find a way to effectively dispute your parking ticket,

"Summertime in the City" by Nadia Quyyum

those who can master the strategies of rhetoric are better equipped when presenting their arguments.

When you read or write an argument, search out the *rhetorical situation*. The Rhetorical Model consists of four elements: author, audience, text, and context. By considering all three sides of the triangle, you arrive at an understanding of the *context* of a particular argument.

If you consider each side of this triangle more fully, you develop more convincing arguments. When you read, listen to, or construct your own arguments, ask the following questions regarding author, audience, and text:

Writer or Speaker (Author):
- Who is the author? What gives him or her credibility with the audience?
- Is the author an expert? What does the author do to establish credibility (ethos)?
- In what ways does the author try to create *common ground*?
- Is the author trying to persuade the audience? Does he or she want the audience to take action?

Reader or Viewer (Audience):
- Who is the target audience? How do you know?
- What background knowledge does the audience already have? What has the author assumed about the audience's knowledge? What does the author provide as a way to inform the perceived "lack" of knowledge held by the audience?
- How do rhetorical appeals (ethos, logos, and pathos) affect the audience?

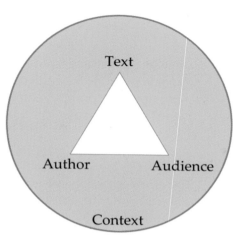

Text (Purpose and Subject):
- What kind of text has the author created? Oral? Written? Visual?
- Which specific genre constitutes this text (letter, speech, blog, video, social networking post, etc.)?
- What is the purpose of the text, and what is the audience expected to think or do?
- How are the claims presented? What kinds of evidence does the author present in support of his or her claims?
- What affect does the text have on you?

Applying the Rhetorical Situation

What makes Dr. Martin Luther King's "I have a Dream" speech so compelling to his listeners? What rhetorical devices does the reverend use in "Letter from Birmingham Jail"? These two examples depict effective oral and written argument and, what's more, they illustrate Dr. King's understanding of the power of *rhetoric*.

> Visit the companion web site to the *Guide to First Year Writing*. Here you will find a link to Dr. King's speech and one to a full text of read his "Letter from Birmingham Jail."
>
> 1. Create a *summary* of what you understand about both texts.
>
> 2. *Analyze* what you know about the author, the audiences, and the texts.
>
> 3. Discuss how Dr. King's argument in both texts gains strength through his consideration of the three components of the *rhetorical triangle*.

RHETORICAL APPEALS

In his treatise *On Rhetoric*, Aristotle discusses three appeals a writer should use when constructing effective arguments: *ethos*, *logos*, and *pathos*. These appeals pull on the audience's imagination and emotions. Aristotle calls these appeals "proofs," and he writes about their persuasive abilities with regard to audience.

Ethos

The *ethos* appeal consists of an argument made through the author's *character*. In order to construct an effective argument, the author must make the audience believe, respect, and trust him or her. The author's character thus forms part of the persuasive appeal. One question a reader may ask when evaluating the ethos of an author is: *What credibility does the author have allowing him or her to pose and support this argument?* The author's personality, reputation, and ability to appear trustworthy are key elements in this appeal. According to Aristotle, ethos consists of four elements:

1. The virtue or moral character of the author.
2. The goodwill created by the author toward the audience.
3. The practical wisdom, or common sense displayed by the author.
4. The disinterestedness, which is the extent to which the author conveys that he or she does not have an ulterior motive in making the argument.

In order to enhance your ethos, you must act with *decorum*. That means that you must act as the audience expects you to act; you must demonstrate yourself as authentic, informed, honest, mature, formal, compassionate, and engaging. Doing extensive, ethical research certainly contributes to your ethos. Paying attention to details such as grammar, mechanics, and manuscript form in your writing enhances your ethos as well. Another way to enhance your ethical stance is by using a tone that conveys passion about your subject matter without being overbearing or strident. Sometimes, when we feel strongly about something, we use emotionally charged language and a judgmental tone that could offend some audience members. For example, instead of saying,

"Climate-change deniers are just plain ignorant. Why can't they see the facts?"

A better approach might be something like this statement:

"Before being so quick to dismiss the scientific evidence of climate change, the deniers should ask themselves why all of the world's top scientists and international policymakers are convinced of humankind's destructive effects on the environment."

Appeals based on ethos are not confined to any one statement or element of an argument. In order to make an ethical argument, each element must contribute to the overall effect. As you will find in *Chapter Four: Research and Documentation*, the evidence you use to support your claims represents a form of ethos. Your word choice, grammar, tone, personal examples, expertise in the topic area, and method of delivery (a scholarly paper versus a web blog) also enhances your argument's ethical appeal.

Pathos

The word *pathos* has cousins in the words "sympathy," "empathy," "pathetic," and "pathology." People act on their emotions. You might change their minds through reason, but you get them to act based on your ability to tap into their compassion, anger, empathy, idealism, and joy. When you tell a story that evokes memories and tears, when you paint a picture with words that evokes visions of a better world, you are using the pathos appeal. In order to accomplish the goal of persuasion, you must know what your audience will respond to, what will captivate them and spur them into action. What does your audience desire? Fear? Doubt? Believe? Hope?

Including narratives, metaphors, humor, images, and carefully chosen words and phrases enables you to make effective appeals based on pathos. For example, using words associated with deep-seated feelings and affiliations will cause the audience to believe you and become inspired by your words. Think of words like "liberty," "equality," "justice," "family," "patriotism," "reform," and "prosperity." These words evoke images dear to many hearts in the United States. For instance, consider the difference between the terms "same-sex marriage" and "marriage equality." What is the difference between "terrorist" and "freedom fighter?" or "traitor" and "whistleblower?"

The use of pathos-driven language may *feel* manipulative, in a way. Have you ever watched a commercial that made you cry? Picture images on a television screen of little children who appear sickly and hungry. Add to these images sad background music and cutaway shots of children crying alone in the corner of a sparsely furnished room. How do these images affect you? Are you willing to do whatever is asked of you at the end of the commercial? If the commercial asks you to send just ten cents a day to a corporation who promises to feed these children, are you more apt to send the money after seeing the images? The manipulative (or persuasive) nature of pathos makes this rhetorical appeal especially powerful.

In order to use pathos appeals optimally, you must sympathize or empathize with your audience. Mirror your audience's emotions. When you encounter a friend who is sad, do you look sad, too, or do you say, "Cheer up!" Your friend would rather you commiserate with him or her, correct? Talking down to people does not work. Commiserating with them is much more effective. This reaction of sympathy (or empathy, if you actually *do* feel their pain) serves as a foundation from which you move the audience toward feeling the way you want them to feel. You serve as an emotional barometer for them, modeling the reaction you want. You start with sympathy/empathy and move toward identification and action.

"Arrival" by Marissa Graziano

Logos

Logos concerns most of what we would call the proof or evidence in an argument.

In Greek, the word has gained a number of meanings, including "word," "plea," "opinion," "speech," or "reasoned discourse." Aristotle argued that logos formed the most important consideration for an orator. He discusses deductive reasoning strategies such as using expert opinion (testimony), as well as a set of memory joggers called "commonplaces," which you will read about in a later section of this chapter. Here is an example of a "syllogism," an argument an attorney might make:

> To qualify as a "citizen" of a state for purposes of diversity jurisdiction, a party must (1) currently reside in that state and (2) intend to remain there indefinitely. (*Major premise; states a rule of law.*) Here, the plaintiff does not currently reside in North Carolina. (*Minor premise; makes a statement of fact.*) Therefore, the plaintiff cannot be a "citizen" of North Carolina for jurisdictional purposes. (*Conclusion; correctly applies the law to the facts.*)[1]

In order to make a proper logos appeal, you do not have to devise sophisticated syllogisms like the one above. You just need to provide facts, statistics, examples, and statements from experts, documented carefully; furthermore, you must put pieces of evidence together in such a way that your conclusion arises inevitably from your evidence.

To use an appeal based on logos means that the text contains a clear claim or thesis that is substantiated with reasons and evidence, and that all of the material is presented in an internally consistent, well-organized manner. Typically, a writer or speaker will proceed from the weakest point to the strongest, from the strongest to the weakest, or will compare different solutions to argue for the best outcome, or will show cause and effect through a chronological examination of events. Since an audience best remembers what they hear first and last, most rhetoric texts suggest placing the strongest support for your argument near the beginning and end of your piece. Together, the content and the organization (logical form) contribute to the logos of the argument. Each of the three appeals—ethos, pathos, and logos—works together to create a cumulative effect.

---

1. You can read more about this example of syllogism in "Logic and Legal Reasoning: A Guide for Law Students," online at http://www.unc.edu/~ramckinn/Documents/NealRameeGuide.pdf

Applying Rhetorical Appeals

Go back to Dr. Martin Luther King's "Letter from Birmingham Jail"

1. Consider your analysis of the rhetorical situation.
2. Using three different highlighting markers, indicate where Dr. King uses *ethos*, *pathos*, and *logos*.
3. Discuss the effect these appeals have on his intended audience.
4. Now argue how the appeals help to create and support the argument he presents.

RHETORICAL FALLACIES:

As this chapter illustrates, the use of rhetorical appeals contributes to the overall effectiveness of your argument. However, if you use an appeal incorrectly or unethically, you intentionally or not create a fallacious argument. Fallacies are misleading or unsound (unreasonable) arguments. Rhetorical fallacies are everywhere—we encounter them every day. Since there are three *rhetorical appeals*, fallacies are divided among them. Keep in mind, though, that the rhetorical fallacies, like the appeals themselves, often overlap. For example, a fallacy might simultaneously use faulty logic and unreasonably advance the writer's character, so it might be both a logical and ethical fallacy.

Ethical Fallacies

Ethical fallacies unfairly or unreasonably advance the character or credibility of the author.

False Authority. The "False Authority" fallacy asks audiences to agree with the author's claims based on testimony by the author or by someone who does not have the authority to advance the claim, i.e., someone who does not have expert qualification in advising on the matter.

Example: "Michael Jordan drinks Gatorade, so electrolytes must be good for you."

Using Authority Instead of Evidence. In this fallacy, the writer insists that the audience believe him or her without any proof. First-person narratives, when produced as though they are irrefutable, fall prey to the essentialist claim that no one can argue with personal experience, no matter how prejudiced or limited the perspective.

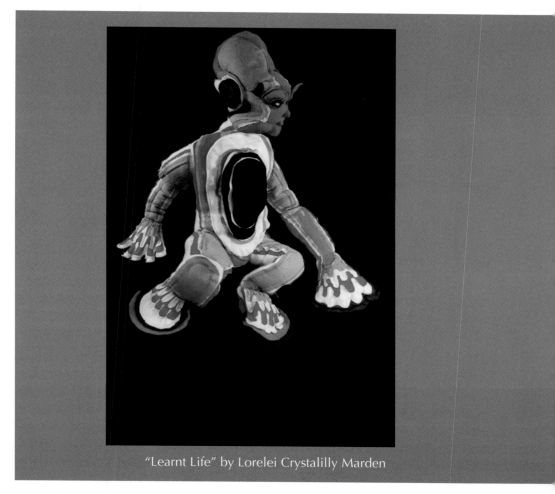

"Learnt Life" by Lorelei Crystalilly Marden

Example: "Believe me; no one could have won in an election against such an opponent."

Guilt by Association. The writer calls into question an opponent's character by pointing out that person's friends or associates.

Example: "John must be a snob. He's on the debating team, which is full of snobs."[2]

Dogmatism. Dogmatism shuts down debate by insisting that the author's views are the only acceptable ones.

Example: "Well, I believe nuclear energy is clean, and that's that."

---

2   From http://online.santarosa.edu/presentation/page/?36896

Moral Equivalence. The "moral equivalence" fallacy equates a minor issue to a major moral crisis.

Example: "'An anti-smoking moralist barks: 'Smoking cigarettes is nothing short of suicide—the smoker is willingly killing himself.' National anti-smoking campaigns often avoid the moral argument because the public understands that smoking is a personal choice that probably will not impact one's morality."[3]

Ad Hominem. In Latin, *ad hominem* means "to the man." In order to avoid dealing with the issue, writers will often attack an opponent personally. Many of these abuses involve the use of labels or loaded words that have negative connotations in the minds of the target audience. This fallacy often appears in mudslinging attack ads during political campaigns.

Example: "The lifestyle of a political candidate is addressed in the press, rather than the candidate's ideas and platform issues."[4]

The "You, too!" Fallacy. This abuse of ethos sets up a new moral standard, generating an example of someone else's breaking of the original rule. In other words, "Somebody else did it, so it is okay for me to do it, too." The arguer's words either contradict an earlier position on the issue, or the arguer's words and actions do not match.

Example: "Peter: 'Based on the arguments I have presented, it is evident that it is morally wrong to use animals for food or clothing.' Bill: 'But you are wearing a leather jacket and you have a roast beef sandwich in your hand! How can you say that using animals for food and clothing is wrong!'"[5]

The "Who Says So?" Fallacy. This abuse of ethics also provides a variety of the Ad Hominem attack. The ethical problem relates to *who* says something more than *what* the person says. In other words, the very source of the argument is given by the opponent as a reason not to believe it.

Example: "Look who's talking. You say I shouldn't become an alcoholic because it will hurt me and my family, yet you yourself are an alcoholic, so your argument can't be worth listening to."[6]

Straw Man. This fallacy sets up a "straw man," or false opponent, which misrepresents the opponent's claims. In this way, the writer appears to defeat the second party/opponent, while in reality only defeating a weaker, inaccurate version of the opponent's argument.

3   From http://ksuweb.kennesaw.edu/~shagin/logfal-analysis-moralequiv.htm
4   From http://www.uta.edu/english/SH/Fallacies.htm
5   From http://www.nizkor.org/features/fallacies/ad-hominem-tu-quoque.html
6   From http://www.iep.utm.edu/fallacy/#TuQuoque

Example: *"Opponent*: 'Because of the killing and suffering of Indians that followed Columbus's discovery of America, the City of Atlanta should declare that Columbus Day will no longer be observed in our city.'

Speaker: 'This is ridiculous, fellow members of the city council. It's not true that every person who came to America from another country somehow oppressed the Indians. I say we should continue to observe Columbus Day, and vote down this resolution that will make the City of Atlanta the laughing stock of the nation.'"[7]

Emotional Fallacies

Emotional fallacies unfairly appeal to the audience's emotions, generally by using emotions to distort or ignore logic. These fallacies often appear in political propaganda and in advertising.

Sentimental Appeals. This fallacy uses emotions to draw the audience away from facts.

Example: "Millions of cats and dogs undergo cruel, invasive surgery each year to reduce their population. This horrific treatment of spaying and neutering should not be practiced."

Red Herring. A "red herring" is designed to distract the audience from the real argument. The name comes from fox hunting, where servants would drag dried, smoked herring (a fish that has a red color when dried) across the trail of a fox to hide the scent from the hounds.

Example: *Student*: 'The opinions of the students are completely ignored in the process of determining both curricular changes and social programs. The students should have a much greater voice in campus governance, because we have a very great stake in this institution, and we think that we have a positive contribution to make.'

Professor: 'The faculty are the ones who need a greater voice. Professors can be fired without explanation, and they have no control over who is promoted or given tenure. Their opinions about budgetary allotments are completely ignored. Why aren't you concerned about the injustice the faculty is experiencing?'[8]

Scare Tactics. The writer tries to convince the audience that if his or her plan is not adopted, something dire will happen.

---

7   From http://www.iep.utm.edu/fallacy/#StrawMan
8   From http://www.txstate.edu/philosophy/resources/fallacy-definitions/Red-Herring.html

Example: "*David*: 'My father owns the department store that gives your newspaper fifteen percent of all its advertising revenue, so I'm sure you won't want to publish any story of my arrest for spray painting the college.'

Newspaper editor: 'Yes, David, I see your point. The story really isn't newsworthy.'"9

Slippery Slope. Similar to the Scare Tactic, the Slippery Slope argues that one thing will lead to another, with calamitous results.

Example: "*Mom*: 'Those look like bags under your eyes. Are you getting enough sleep?'

Jeff: 'I had a test and stayed up late studying.'

Mom: 'You didn't take any drugs, did you?'

Jeff: 'Just caffeine in my coffee, like I always do.'

Mom: 'Jeff! You know what happens when people take drugs! Pretty soon the caffeine won't be strong enough. Then you will take something stronger, maybe someone's diet pill or an energy drink. Then, you will try something even stronger. Eventually, you will be doing methamphetamines. Then you will be a cocaine addict! So, don't drink that coffee.'"10

Bandwagon Appeals. This fallacy plays upon the audience's need for belonging and affiliation. "Jumping on the bandwagon" means going along with what other people are doing.

Example: "Everyone who's anyone has tattoos. If you don't have a tattoo, how will you fit in with the cool people?"

Either/Or Choices (False Dilemma). This fallacy reduces a complex issue to only two possible choices, when in actuality there are likely several other choices.

All complex issues have a number of varying perspectives.

Example: In his book *Hostages to Fortune*, David Newnham describes a woman using an either/or (false dilemma) fallacy: "Gerda Reith is convinced that superstition can be a positive force. 'It gives you a sense of control by making you think you can work out what's going to happen next,' she says. 'And it also makes you feel lucky. And to take a risk or to enter into a chancy situation, you really have to believe in your own luck. In that sense, it's a very useful way of thinking, because the alternative is fatalism,

---

9   From http://www.iep.utm.edu/fallacy/#ScareTactic
10 From http://www.iep.utm.edu/fallacy/#SlipperySlope

which is to say, "Oh, there's nothing I can do." At least superstition makes people do things.'"[11]

False Need. This fallacy plays upon desires by creating a need and then promising to fill it.

Example: "You must have the latest in smart phones. You deserve the best; people will think of you as someone who is tech savvy."

Logical Fallacies

Logical fallacies depend upon faulty informal and formal logic.

Hasty Generalization. The author draws a conclusion from insufficient evidence.

This fallacy uses faulty inductive reasoning, establishing a conclusion from too few examples.

Example: "I will never shop at that store again. The customer service is terrible. Once, one of the clerks rolled her eyes at me when I asked a question."

Post Hoc Ergo Propter Hoc (After This, Therefore Because of This). Just because something happens after something else does not mean that the first event causes the second. The Romans called this slip-up *"Post hoc, ergo propter hoc,"* or "After this, therefore because of this."

Example: "Two years ago, the school system cut its funding by 30 percent. Last year, teacher attrition doubled and student dropout rates increased by 20 percent. Clearly, funding cuts have a dire effect on retention of teachers and students."

Cum Hoc Ergo Propter Hoc (With This, Therefore Because of This). This fallacy assumes causation where none may in fact exist. Just because two things coincide does not mean one causes the other.

Example: "He sometimes behaves violently when I am around him. I don't know what it is that I am doing to make him become so violent."[12]

Non Sequitur. Latin for "it does not follow," the *Non Sequitur* Fallacy makes a statement that does not logically relate to what came before it. The author may have left out an important link in the chain of logic. That

---

11 Quoted in http://www.fallacyfiles.org/eitheror.html

12 From http://www.outofthefog.net/Treatment/CumHocErgoPropterHoc.html

is, the conclusion the arguer makes can only be supported by weak or irrelevant reasons.

Example: "Nuclear disarmament is a risk, but everything in life involves a risk. Every time you drive in a car you are taking a risk. If you're willing to drive in a car, you should be willing to have disarmament."[13]

Equivocation. This fallacy obscures the whole truth by revealing only a partial truth. In court, the oath "tell the truth, the whole truth, and nothing but the truth" is designed to subvert the possibility of witnesses committing this fallacy. The author committing this fallacy uses a word that proves ambiguous; that is, the word could be interpreted as meaning two different things. In other words, the word shifts meaning within the statement.

Example: "Brad is a nobody, but since nobody is perfect, Brad must be perfect, too."[14]

Begging the Question. The writer restates his or her claim in a different way, appearing to make an argument. Have you ever looked up a word in the dictionary or online, and the definition has the word in it? If so, you have encountered a similar phenomenon, the circular definition or "tautology."

Example of "begging the question": "'Women have rights,' said the Bullfighters Association president. 'But women shouldn't fight bulls because a bullfighter is and should be a man.'"[15]

False Analogy. In this fallacy, the author draws an analogy between two things that are not comparable. We sometimes call this "comparing apples to oranges."

Example: "Clogged arteries require surgery to clear them; our clogged highways require equally drastic measures."[16]

Stacked Evidence. This fallacy entails framing a debate in such a way that all discourse not friendly to the arguer's position is precluded. In other words, the writer of the Stacked Evidence Fallacy sets up the argument in such a way that his or her points are the only ones discussed and he or she fails to address any counterarguments.

Example: "TV is beneficial because it offers PBS, The History Channel, and the news."[17]

---

13 From http://www.iep.utm.edu/fallacy/#NonSequitur

14 From http://www.iep.utm.edu/fallacy/#Equivocation

15 From http://www.iep.utm.edu/fallacy/#BeggingtheQuestion

16 From http://ksuweb.kennesaw.edu/~shagin/logfal-analysis-falseanalogy.htm

17 From http://www.uta.edu/english/SH/Fallacies.htm

You will discover that fallacies of all three kinds are common in arguments. As a rational and critical thinker, you must think about and analyze every bit of data that comes your way.

Finding and Analyzing Rhetorical Fallacies

Find a print advertisement, a radio spot, or a television commercial and analyze the rhetorical fallacies on which the "argument" depends.

1. Conduct a rhetorical analysis of the advertisement. Start with the rhetorical triangle.
2. What rhetorical appeals does the advertisement use? Is the appeal effective in bolstering the argument?
3. Discuss the advertisement's use of rhetorical fallacies (there may be more than one). How do the fallacies undermine the intent of the argument?

CREATING THE RHETORICAL POSITION: THESIS STATEMENT

All arguments center on a clearly defined and directly stated *claim*. The sentence that poses this central claim is called the *thesis statement*. When locating the thesis statement, you should ask "What is this author's main point? What is the author trying to prove?" Effective thesis statements leave little room for inference. A thesis statement also provides a "road map" of sorts for the argument: it will state the main point and includes the *how so?* and *so what?* and *why is this important?* Thesis, then, is crucial to the structure of your argument, which is why you will often find the thesis in the opening section (introduction) to an argumentative paper or speech. Thesis statements take a stance and they pose a supportable argument. They also use specific language and focus on a topic that allows for a discussion. For instance, stating "We should stop world hunger" isn't *debatable*. How many people would disagree with the need to curb world hunger? However, arguing American tax-payer money should go to fund a world-wide program to stop hunger *is debatable*.

A strong thesis focuses on a subject that has two sides (a topic that provides an oppositional point of view). The thesis should express only one main point and provide the subclaims for that point. Be sure, too, your thesis is "appropriate" for the assignment length, mode of delivery, and audience.

"Held Together by a Thread" by Stephanie Liebetreu

To create a thesis statement, you will need to first start with your central *claim.*

> *Social Media*

Now articulate what you plan to argue about this broad topic:

> *Social media has altered how we interact with people.*

You must go from a broad argument to a more specific one. The above statement should answer the questions: *How so? Why is this important?*

> *Social media is detrimental to adolescent social development.*

Check to make sure this topic is relevant, debatable, and provable (meaning, can you find the evidence you need to support the claim)? Next, focus on the specifics of the claim by writing down your subclaims:

> *Cyber bullying*

> *Virtual relationships differ from in-person relationships.*

> *Teens are not developing the social skills they need to be part of their familial and community relationships.*

At this point, you might go to the GSU library site to check on the number of articles, books, and media resources available to you on this topic. Now it is time to pull the statement together:

> *Parents should restrict adolescents' access to social media because it makes them susceptible to cyber bullying, it favors virtual relationships over in person interactions, and it decreases their ability to develop the social skills needed to be part of the community.*

OR

> *Social media platforms such as Facebook and Twitter undermine an adolescent's necessary communal-based development by favoring virtual-world realationships and, therefore, omit the development of social skills needed to interact with people in face-to-face reality.*

This argumentative, supportable, and directly stated sentence allows (provides the "road map") for an extended discussion of the three subclaims listed above. Regardless of the *model of argument* you use, strong thesis statements ground by directly stating the purpose and the main points.

Applying the Rhetorical Position

> *Social media platforms such as Facebook and Twitter undermine an adolescent's necessary communal-based development by favoring virtual-world relationships and, therefore, omit the development of social skills needed to interact with people in face-to-face reality.*
>
> *Using "social media" as the initial claim, work through the steps provided above to create an oppositional point of view to this thesis statement.*

ARGUMENT MODELS

The Classical Model

Of all the argument models, you are no doubt most familiar with the Classical Model. The five-paragraph themes you wrote in grade school were modeled on the classical form of argument. As more advance writers, however, you will develop your arguments beyond the five-paragraph structure. The five-paragraph structure provides a good organizational model. Your thesis and research, though, may require more lengthy sections. Most of the arguments produced by ancient Greek and Roman orators were in the forum of law courts and legislative assemblies, with orators interested primarily in proving truth from the facts at hand in the case. Thus, the Classical Model privileges logos-based appeals. The Classical structure consists of the following elements:

Introduction. In this section, the author announces the subject and purpose of the argument. In the introduction, the author answers the "so what?" question (i.e., the argument's significance) and establishes *ethos* with the audience.

Narratio. In the *narratio* or background section, the author provides a background story for the issue at hand, in other words, what is known as fact about the issue. The author provides an overview of the issue's history and the various perspectives surrounding the controversy, outlining the *context* of the issue. Usually, at the end of the *narratio*, the author provides the *propositio*, a summary of the issues or a statement of the claim. We typically call this statement the *thesis*.

Partitio. This portion of the model's structure outlines what will follow, in accordance with the nature of the stated issue. In other words, the author provides an overview of the sections of the text: that is, the reasons that the claim is valid. Sometimes, an author combines the *propositio* and *partitio* in the *narratio*.

Confirmatio. Forming the heart of the argument, the *confirmatio* provides the evidence for each of the reasons supporting the claim. Thus, the claim, given in the *narratio*, and the reasons, given in the *partitio*, are expounded upon in the *confirmatio*, with ample, credible, relevant evidence.

Refutatio. In the *refutatio*, the author addresses the counterarguments to his or her claim and refutes them one by one. Both the *confirmatio* and the *refutatio* use the *logos* appeal as the predominant method for making the argument.

Peroratio. In the *peroratio*, or summation, the author concludes the argument through reiterating the claim and making a strong call to action. Pathos appeals constitute the privileged appeal in the *peroratio*. Here, the author returns to the "so what?" question and hammers home the most important points, demonstrating beyond a doubt both the significance and the feasibility of the claims he or she has made, as well as what the audience should "take away" from the argument.

"One Step at a Time" by James Supreme

If you remember these simple facets of the Classical Model, you will be well on your way to making effective use of this structure:

- Explain why your argument is important, establishing your ethos.
- Give the context through telling the back story. Make a claim.
- Give the reasons your claim is valid. Use logos.
- Provide the evidence for each reason. Use logos.
- Address the possible counterarguments. Use logos.
- Summarize the main points and reiterate the call to action. Use pathos.

The Rogerian Model

The Rogerian Model emerged from the conflict resolution work of American psychologist Carl Rogers. Dr. Rogers developed his model in order to help the author build "common ground" in addressing audiences that are not receptive to the message, or even openly hostile to it. If you are dealing with a controversial issue, and you think you may be arguing an unpopular position, you may find the Rogerian Model useful and effective. In simplest terms, the Rogerian argument reverses the main sections of the Classical model, foregrounding the counterarguments in order to build consensus between the author and the audience. This model privileges pathos and ethos over logos, but logos still provides important support to the argument. Remember that in Rogerian argument, the goal is to get the audience to consider a viewpoint that does not align with their own, so knowing the audience's characteristics becomes especially crucial. Rogers emphasized "empathic listening," which involves a deep knowledge of the audience's needs, desires, and prejudices, as well as their baseline knowledge regarding the issue. Additionally, the Rogerian structure centers on an approach to argument based on consensus. Rogerian arguments do not aim to "win," but rather to present a point of view in a manner that allows for consideration. The following sections outline the elements of the Rogerian structure.

Introduction. State the problem you hope to resolve. By presenting the issue as a problem that can be solved, you increase the chance that the audience will see the problem as well.

Summary of Opposing Views. As neutrally and diplomatically as possible, state the views of people with whom you disagree. Make sure that you provide an accurate assessment of those views. By showing that you can listen without judging and can give a fair hearing to the other sides of the issue, you demonstrate that your own views are worth attention. You create ethos with your audience in this way.

Statement of Understanding. Also known as the "statement of validity," this section demonstrates an understanding of the validity of other views. Here, you explain the circumstances in which the opposing views are valid. Which parts of the argument would you concede to be legitimate? Under what conditions are these parts legitimate? This statement allows you to qualify your argument by not making sweeping, insupportable statements.

Statement of Your Position. Now that the audience understands that you are willing to listen to and concede their views, they will now receive your argument. Here, you make your claim by stating your position on the issue.

Statement of Contexts. Describe situations and contexts in which you hope your views will be respected. By outlining specific contexts, you imply your understanding that not everyone will agree with you at all times. Opponents, however, are invited to agree with parts of your argument in the effort toward building common ground.

Statement of Benefits. End your argument on a positive note by expressing to the audience how they will benefit from considering your argument and acting accordingly. Not only does this technique appeal to their self-interest, but it also allows you to move forward into future goals and actions.

Remember these essential points about Rogerian argumentation:

- Use this model when the audience does not agree with you.
- Build common ground/consensus predominantly with ethos and pathos.
- Foreground counterarguments.
- Work up to your thesis.
- End on a positive note with explaining benefits to audience.

The Toulmin Model

Stephen Toulmin, a British philosopher, developed this model to handle arguments based on probability rather than absolute truth. The ancients who developed the Classical Model operated on the notion that philosophy must deal with absolute truth. As Aristotle contributed to the field of rhetoric, however, the emphasis shifted to probability and likelihood, so the writer argues the case that best fits the truth. The Toulmin Model provides not only a structure for you to use to organize your argument, but also a checklist for revision. Using this list of elements, you can analyze the aspects of your argument in order to identify weak parts as well as to improve the stronger parts of your work.

The following represents the six elements of the Toulmin Model, adapted from the GSU English website for Rhetoric and Composition:[18]

- **Claims**: There are several different types of claims: claims of fact, claims of definition, claims of cause, claims of value, and claims of policy. An author may use any one or more of these claims to introduce the issue and to establish the case.
- **Data:** Information an author uses to support claims.

---

18 Handout for 1101 on Models of Argument: http://www.rhetcomp.gsu.edu/~bgu/1101/models. html

- **Warrant:** The assumption made by a writer in order for the claim to be true. The warrant connects the claim to the data.
- **Backing:** What the author uses to support the warrant.
- **Rebuttal:** The portion of the argument in which the author considers the opposing viewpoint and refutes it.
- **Qualifier:** Language that qualifies the claims of the author; qualifiers allow for probability rather than absolute truth, giving the argument a stronger chance of being accepted by and acted upon by the audience.

The Toulmin Model enables you to analyze your argument to find its weaknesses and strengthen them. Remember that the three basic parts consist of the claim, the grounds, and the warrant. The grounds support the claim, and the backing supports the warrant. In order to acknowledge the contingent and contextual nature of the argument, the rebuttal acknowledges the counterarguments. The qualifier shapes the claim in order to allow for the counterarguments. The ideal argument has all six components.

Toulmin Argument Example: "Single-use Plastic Bags Should Be Banned"

Single-use plastic shopping bags should be banned in the U.S. (claim) because they contribute to the pollution of our environment (data). They cannot be reused according to law or store policy. If they are reused for other purposes, they become soiled and wind up in landfills. Only one percent of the bags placed in recycling bins are ever recycled by processing plants (data). Whether the bags end up in the landfill or are burned in incinerators, they emit toxins into our environment (data). These toxins are harmful to soil, water, and air (warrant). Burning the bags emits toxic gases and increases the level of VOCs (volatile organic compounds) into the air, while landfills take up precious soil resources by holding the plastic in the earth, where it emits toxins as it decomposes (backing). The "trash vortex," a soup of plastic goo floating in the Pacific, covers a water area the size of Texas and kills marine life at every level of the food chain (backing). Most metropolitan areas could institute the ban and enforce it, but smaller cities and towns might not have as many resources (qualifier). A ban would take some getting used to on the part of retailers and consumers (rebuttal), but the effort would pay off by decreasing the number of bags polluting the environment. A number of U.S. cities (Los Angeles, Seattle) and one state (Hawaii) have instituted the ban with positive results.

CLAIM
single-use plastic bags
should be banned

REASON
because they contribute
to the pollution of the
environment

QUALIFIER
most metropolitan
areas could
institute the ban
effectively

DATA
almost all
bags wind up
in landfills,
incinerators,
or littering the
landscape; they
emit toxins

WARRANT
toxins are harmful to soil, air,
and water

BACKING
burning bags emits VOCs into air;
bags in landfills poison soil; the
trash vortex in the Pacific kills
marine life

REBUTTAL
the ban will take some
adjustment for retailers and
consumers

MAKING ORAL ARGUMENTS

Argument is an ancient mode of communication. In the invention stages of argumentative practices, most notions concerning rhetoric and the development and delivery of argument applied to orators. You may be asked in your first year writing classes to present your work in an oral or group presentation. In addition to the more formal presentation assignment, your instructor may ask you to work in groups, which requires you to vocalize ideas to your peers. As a student, you will articulate your position in both written and oral formats.

When constructing oral arguments, keep in mind Cicero's five canons: *invention, arrangement, style, memory, and delivery.* Cicero designed his system after legal and political oratory. These five canons of oral rhetoric are still useful today; and they connect to the discussion of writing as well. Imagine the writing process: prewriting, drafting, revising, editing, and publishing as a mirror image to the five categories classical rhetoricians such as Cicero adopted for oration. When crafting an oral argument, pick a topic and figure out what you want to say about it; decide which order of topics is best; create the most engaging, convincing style for the audience and purpose; write your thoughts and research on notecards or in a computer-based presentation format; and present the material to the audience in an authoritative manner (ethos).

Invention

Your instructor may call invention strategies *heuristics*. In Greek, the word "heuristic" refers to a method of finding or discovering ideas or solutions to problems. Heuristics are techniques to help you figure out what you want to include in your argument. Here are brief descriptions of several basic strategies.

Commonplaces

Commonplaces are topics that we use to make arguments. The word *topic* comes from the Greek *topoi*, which means "a place." The term "commonplace" echoes this notion of location, in its connotation of being a place from which to craft an argument. In order to know the best commonplaces, we must understand our audience's needs, desires, and background knowledge. If we know our audience values the notion of family and home, we can use the language of family and home to make our arguments. Other commonplaces help us divide and organize our topics, enabling us to move into the canon of arrangement. For example, the technique of comparing and contrasting proves to be a familiar way to talk about an issue; analyzing similarities and differences, therefore, forms one commonplace.

Artistic Proofs

Artistic proofs develop from the speaker's own mind. An individual develops thoughts from prior knowledge and ethical conviction, then fashions these thoughts into a logical structure of argument. In this way, the author can explore and narrow the topic, create a thesis, and determine which ideas should be conveyed to the audience.

These proofs form the only purely invented ones, and Aristotle considered them vitally important. The artistic proofs can be further categorized as deductive and inductive reasoning. A scientist uses deductive reasoning when she has a hypothesis and tests it in an experiment. She works from the general principle to the specific case. A literary critic uses induc-

"Bernice King" by Joshua Yu

tive reasoning when he collects details of a poet's life through her poetry, and derives a theory about the poet based on these various examples. He works from the specific examples to a general principle. No one method proves better than the other, but in making an argument, we find it useful to think about how best to proceed with our reasoning, and use that model to guide us. See the chapter on analysis in this text for more on deductive and inductive reasoning.

Inartistic Proofs

While artistic proofs originate, like art itself, from the author, inartistic proofs originate outside the speaker's mind. Anything that is not invented through careful thought and reasoning, including any material from prima-ry or secondary sources, is considered an inartistic proof. Using statistics, expert testimony, surveys, primary documents, or other types of research can also help us make effective arguments. In order to know what to say about an issue, we need to know what has already been said. What are the various viewpoints on this issue? How and by whom have these ideas been presented?

Performing research must support our invention process rather than leading it. Consider research a discovery process. Ask questions, and let the research help you arrive at possible answers for those questions. The questions themselves, and even the topic, may transform in the research and writing process, which is a natural and desirable development. Often, when people research a topic, they seek out sources that support their own, already set-in-stone viewpoint, rather than carefully considering other viewpoints and synthesizing the arguments with their original thoughts. The best arguments form sophisticated syntheses of both artistic and inartistic proofs.

Arrangement

Once a composer has invented material for an argument, he or she must arrange that material into the most logical, effective order. This part of the writing process, and the second canon of rhetoric, is known as *arrangement*. The arrangement canon applies not only to ordering the parts of an argument in a model such as the classical structure, but also to ordering ideas in sentences and the construction of sentences and paragraphs that flow well and that make sense to the audience. Therefore, when you arrange your material from your own mind as well as from sources, you can refer to the argument models to give you a sense of the big picture.

For example, as mentioned in the section on Rogerian argument, you might prefer to state counterarguments first if you know the audience may be initially unwilling to accept your claim. You can arrange your points using the Rogerian model.

In the next sections, two of the most common and useful arrangement strategies are presented: amplification and parallelism. The first one applies to the overall structure of the argument, and the second applies more commonly to the words, phrases, and sentences within the structure.

Amplification

In rhetoric, *amplification* refers to addressing the parts of an argument structure in the most effective fashion. Generally, the term refers to the layering of data to create overwhelming evidence for the claim of the argument. Therefore, the use of multiple facts, statistics, examples, and expert testimonials *amplifies* (or makes *louder*) the points made in the argument.

For instance, the author might amplify an argument against the use of plastic shopping bags by using the following strategy:

"*Not only* does the use of plastic shopping bags contribute to the tonnage of solid waste in landfills, *but* it *also* adds to the plastic waste that gets carried into rivers and oceans, poisoning wildlife." This particular use is also known as the "But wait, there's more" pitch.[19]

The *digression* also amplifies the text if it helps to prove the argument. A digression is a kind of rhetorical tangent that serves both to divert attention away from the possible objections as well as to subtly emphasize the point. In one of his most famous orations, Cicero defended a poet named Archias, whose Roman citizenship was in dispute. Cicero delivered a long speech in praise of literature, which distracted the audience from the issue of citizenship and highlighted the importance of Archias's profession: poetry. Cicero cleverly won the argument.

Finally, *ordinatio* means ordering or numbering the divisions of an argument so that the audience can follow the author's points.

Example: "When choosing whether to go to war with Iran, we must consider three crucial issues. First, we must consider the financial cost to our national budget, as well as money devoted by all parties to rebuilding the country. Second, we must think of the diplomatic cost, the cost in goodwill to our country in its relationship with other nations. Third and most important, we must privilege the human cost—the physical and mental injuries to both soldiers and civilians in all nations affected by the conflict."

Amplification consists of taking each part of the argument structure and expanding it with ample, accurate, and relevant data so that the argument proves compellingly persuasive.

Parallelism

Parallelism, or parallel structure, concerns either the entire argument structure or a smaller unit within it, such as a sentence. Parallelism is a figure not only of arrangement, but also one of style. Parallelism can be used with other strategies for heightened effect. The following are several examples of parallel structure. In the example about the possibility of war with Iran given above, the three considerations are given in the form of *costs*. They all match in terms of the way that they are framed. Therefore, the points of

---

19 From Jay Heinrichs, Thank You for Arguing: What Aristotle, Lincoln, and Homer Simpson Can Teach Us About Persuasion.

the *confirmatio*, or body of the argument, are parallel. The following examples provide ways to structure sentences for maximum effect.

Style

Invention concerns what will be said. Arrangement addresses the order of the ideas. And style refers to how the ideas will be expressed. Drafting and revising are parts of the writing process in which style emerges as a dominant consideration. The style canon contains so many strategies that it would be impossible to describe them in detail in this short guide. However, a few of the most important aspects of style include the following: diction (word choice), figurative language, correctness, clarity, and level of formality.

The virtues of style described by ancient rhetors include *correctness* of usage and grammar; *clarity* (no ambiguity or obscurity of language); vivid *sensory detail*; *decorum* (propriety); and *ornateness* (beautiful language). Classical rhetors go on to describe the quality of ornateness in detail, focusing primarily on the technique of *metaphor*. They also discuss many other figures of speech, such as *simile*, *personification*, and *analogy*, but often devote the most attention to metaphor.

For example, Aristotle believed that metaphors teach the audience through a *visual* connection between the metaphor and what it refers to. The metaphor creates a figurative or abstract connection that *carries* meaning. In this metaphor, determine which two things are being compared and think about what they have in common: "With this faith we will be able to transform the jangling discords of our nation into a beautiful symphony of brotherhood."—Dr. Martin Luther King, Jr., "I Have a Dream." What is Dr. King trying to teach his audience about humankind through using this metaphor?

The ancient Greeks developed three levels of style: the high or grand style, the middle style, and the low or plain style. The academic arguments you write in your First-Year English classes use predominantly the middle style. You may remember someone—a peer, family member, or teacher—telling you that you must write in a more formal than the way you speak on an everyday basis. The accepted form of our language among academic and professional audiences is called *Standard American English* (SAE), which is a kind of currency for us to use, just like money is a currency. When we use this middle level of language—not slang, but not technical jargon either—we have the greatest chance of being respected and understood by our audiences.

A careful consideration of style will enable you to write skillful, engaging, and persuasive arguments. Refer to a writing handbook for detailed information regarding style. However, practicing your writing "voice" helps more than any other strategy. Your teacher can help you acquire this skill. Once you find your authentic, original voice, you can enhance its effectiveness with techniques such as sensory description and figurative language. Pay attention to places in your argument that seem flat and uninteresting. These are the points at which you need to create a more engaging style.

Memory

Unlike the ancient orators, we no longer have to memorize speeches. Our forms of rhetoric have expanded tremendously, and our technology ensures that whatever we create is both endlessly revisable and permanent. We can change and save whatever we write, draw, or say. However, some of the strategies of the memory canon can still help us today.

Students and practitioners of rhetoric have traditionally kept *common-place books* to help them generate and remember arguments. They would write down topics, quotations, ideas, and other notes in a notebook so that they could refer back to them when creating arguments, much like many writers today. In this way, the canon of memory ties to the canon of invention. The commonplace book helps the rhetor collect and categorize ideas for arguments in a memorable form. We use databases and bookmark websites, but the ancients created commonplace books. No matter which strategy works for you, find a way to record your artistic proofs as well as inartistic proofs you discover in your reading.

Perhaps you have used *mnemonic aids* when you have studied for a test or had to memorize a speech. A mnemonic device works through association, usually of a visual nature. In the ancient Greek and Roman societies, the orator memorized his speech by imagining walking through a building and creating mental associations with objects in the building. Each object would remind him of a portion of his speech. He created a mental path from object to object, and since each object had been associated with a topic, he could remember what he needed to say. For example, if the hall contains a statue of a famous philosopher, he might use an aphorism, or wise saying, from that philosopher. Try leaving mental bread crumbs through a virtual space the next time you need to memorize talking points in a presentation.

While commonplace books and mnemonic devices help the memory of the speaker, the *conclusion* of an argument helps the memory of the audience. Many writers neglect the conclusion, usually because they are tired of writing. However, the power of the conclusion should not be underestimated. This part of your argument helps your audience remember your points. People tend to remember the last thing they see or hear, so the ending of any argument proves vitally important for its impact. Be sure to end with a bang—give your audience a "takeaway"—a colorful and relevant fact or quote, or a call to rhetorical action.

Delivery

Like the canon of style, *delivery* concerns *how* something is said rather than the content of the text. Even though you may not be delivering an oration, you still deliver a paper or a multimedia project to your instructor and your peers. Often, this canon is omitted from texts on rhetoric, but if we think of delivery as *publication*, or submitting written, oral, or visual work, we can still use it as a vital aspect of argumentation.

Delivery varies by the form or *genre* of the text. For example, if you write a traditional MLA-style paper, you might hand in a hard copy to your instructor, or you might email it or submit it in an online portal. In each of these forms, you are *delivering* the text. You might read it to your peers, or they might read it in a peer review session. Oral presentation also constitutes a form of delivery. If you create a PowerPoint, Prezi, website, blog, video, or podcast, you might present these texts to the class in a multimedia presentation. The oral, written, and visual techniques that you use during the delivery of the text contribute to your ethos. In your final draft, consider the importance of proper grammar, usage, mechanics, documentation, and formatting. In order to deliver the text properly, you must revise for content and organization, edit for style and sentence structure, and proofread for mechanics and formatting. Every step is important, and you may loop back through the steps a few times on your way to delivery. Think of the text as your résumé, your elevator speech, and your video interview all rolled into one. You want it to shine, reflecting your brilliance.

CONCLUSION

You have now read about the rhetorical situation, the rhetorical appeals: *ethos, pathos, and logos*, rhetorical fallacies, and models of argumentative structure. You have also reviewed the five canons of rhetoric as they apply to creating arguments for oral presentations. Argument is **not** just about being heard – it is about being understood. Practicing the techniques in this chapter will help you harness the power of argument.

Four

Research and Documentation

■ INTRODUCTION TO RESEARCH

In college writing, you will be expected to think critically; to offer strong, compelling, and appropriate research to advance your arguments; to discern between scholarly and non-scholarly sources in your research; and to write directly and clearly.

Academic writing has conventional practices, like any other endeavor. For example, it is accepted practice that scholars writing in their fields include a "Literature Review" in their academic papers, showing that they are familiar with the works of scholars who have gone before. With effort, the conventions of academic research can be learned, and your research skills will expand and improve with practice.

You do research every day. If you're in the market for a car, you may research online or talk to a knowledgeable family member about which car fits your needs. If your car requires repair, you may consult online reviews to find a trustworthy mechanic near you. Perhaps you've read the nutritional information on the can to find the sugar content of your favorite energy drink or an online medical article about artificial sweeteners. The information-gathering you will do for college research simply builds on these informal research skills.

By the end of ENGL 1101, and throughout ENGL 1102, you will be expected to write a *researched argument paper*. In this type of paper, you will make an argument—a *claim*. Your claim may be an opinion, an interpretation, a policy proposal, or a cause-and-effect statement, among other things. In your paper, you will be expected to:

1. Make a concise, compelling claim (your argument), and
2. Support your argument with evidence gathered from your research.

MLA DOCUMENTATION STYLE

In college writing, you will be expected to *document* all of the research sources you use. Each discipline uses a particular style according to the priorities and nature of their written discourse. The American Psychological Association (APA) style, for example, is used in business, social sciences, and education, and the Chicago Style is used in journalism. In the humanities, such as English Studies, scholars use the documentation style of the Modern Language Association (MLA).

The MLA Handbook for Writers of Research Papers, Seventh Edition provides guidelines for the MLA style of documentation. For detailed information on MLA citation, please visit the *Guide to First-Year Writing* companion Website at www.guidetowriting.gsu.edu.

It will be helpful to review the "MLA Documentation" section of this chapter. But the best way—by far—to get the hang of documentation is to read the model research essays included here and on our Website.

Note how the authors:
1. smoothly incorporate and synthesize research sources into their texts;
2. create end-of-sentence parenthetical citations; and
3. format their Works Cited pages.

If you are like many First-Year students, you may be intimidated by the prospect of thorough scholarly documentation, not only because there are multiple documentation styles that each have their own minute rules to follow, but also because of the looming spectre of plagiarism. First-Year students frequently, and rightfully, worry about using the undocumented words or ideas of others.

Your instructor is here to help you learn modes of documentation. So stop, ask questions, be sure you understand the documentation rules, because scholarly documentation is about our responsibility to acknowledge the work of others and maintain our credibility.

EVALUATING SOURCES

In researching and writing rhetorically, you boost your *ethos*, or credibility as a writer, by synthesizing your personal knowledge with expert knowledge in a field. The question to keep in mind from the very beginning is "How will this source strengthen my argument? Is it truly relevant and timely?" The goal is to find sources that are appropriate, compelling, complete, and expert. For any source, key factors to consider include *aca-*

"Reach for More" by James Supreme

demic credibility, argument, accuracy, and currency. Scholarly journals and books published by university presses carry the most credibility in academic writing. Some popular sources (popular = written by journalists, not by experts in the field) are credible, depending on context; a news item from *The New York Times*, for example, may be a source of accurate, up-to-the-minute data on a topic. Many popular sources that are meant for entertainment—glossy magazines like *Glamour*—are usually not credible as sources in academic writing (depending on your topic, of course). In addition, most instructors discourage citing Wikipedia as a source because its entries are written by volunteers; readers cannot always evaluate the accuracy of entries. Wikipedia articles on your topic, however, can provide excellent bibliographies and links as starting points for your research.

To succeed in academic writing, you must develop a practiced eye for the difference between scholarly and popular sources, and commit to using scholarly sources.

Scholarly Journals

In general scholarly journals:

- Are written for an audience of professors and students in an academic field

- Are published usually by a university press
- Include few, if any, advertisements within the articles
- Make use of highly specialized vocabulary
- Include articles, graphics, tables, charts
- Append an extensive bibliography at the end of each journal article or book

Examples:

JAMA: The Journal of the American Medical Association
(Written by experts in the field of medicine for others in the field.)

The Journal of Economic Theory
(Writer/audience of economics PhDs, researchers, and students.)

American Literature
(Published by Duke University Press for an academic audience.)

Popular Publications

Popular publications generally:
- Are written by journalists or others
- Are published by a news or popular press
- Include glossy or eye-catching color, many photos
- Rely upon non-technical vocabulary
- Do not include bibliographies

Examples:

The Wall Street Journal (Despite "journal" in the title, it is a popular source—a newspaper written by journalists for a wide audience)

The Economist (Written by journalists, full color, with many ads)

PCWorld (Full color, many ads. Written by journalists for a wide audience)

Primary and Secondary Sources

You will also need to know the difference between primary and secondary research.

Primary research involves first-hand interaction with your subject, including interviewing people and analyzing/working with primary sources like diaries, novels and films (rather than working with second-hand *analyses*

"Books" by William Walsh

of these primary sources). Primary sources stand alone in that they are not interpreting anything else. An example of a primary source is *The Diary of a Young Girl* by Anne Frank.

Secondary research materials, on the other hand, interpret and analyze primary sources. Secondary sources include scholarly journal articles, analyses, and biographies, like *Anne Frank: The Biography* by Melissa Müller.

THE VALUE OF A LIBRARY SEARCH; OR, WHY YOU CAN'T "JUST GOOGLE IT"

Google searching returns a world of information—but often not a world of credibility. Say you are researching the history behind Dr. Martin Luther King's "Letter from Birmingham Jail." You Google "Martin Luther King," and you click on the link for www.martinlutherking.org.

As a "dot-org," it's an organization, so it sounds credible. The site is visually orderly, in terms of neatness and layout. At first glance, you think it might be the Martin Luther King Center, or a memorial foundation, or a reputable archive of King's speeches. You read the website heading: "Martin Luther King Jr: A True Historical Examination. A Valuable Resource for Teachers and Students Alike."

Unfortunately, this page is indeed the work of an organization—a supremacist hate group offering their take on King's life and on the accomplishments of African Americans in general. The site has a wealth of hateful statements about African Americans and other groups.

A good rule of thumb:

To be used in an academic paper, a Web source:

1.   must list an author (the above source does not);
2.   must cite its sources, and
3.   should not exist to sell something.

GoogleScholar—not just Google—is an excellent search engine for on-line scholarly articles. What is the downside of GoogleScholar? Unlike a library database search, it doesn't always give the full text of an article; often, you must pay for the article. The good news: Scholarly articles are available free of charge through a GSU Library search.

QUICK-START: SEARCHING THE GSU PULLEN LIBRARY WEBSITE

You can search the Georgia State University Pullen Library website and its wealth of scholarly databases from your personal computer. Go to http://www.library.gsu.edu/ and click "Libraries" and then "University Library." Last year, the library's website was visited 1.7 million times. If you are

http://www.library.gsu.edu

searching for books, the library houses 1.5 million volumes. Whether you are accessing the library from home or from a library computer, use the following steps to complete a simple and quick search.

For Academic Search Complete, click on "A" in Discover's "Databases A to Z" field. Then, click "Academic Search Complete."

Finding Articles in Scholarly Journals

To establish credibility in your academic writing, be sure to find and use peer-reviewed scholarly journal articles in your research. "Peer-reviewed" means that articles have been screened and vetted by experts in the field for reliability and relevance before being published and used by other scholars.

Go to the library webpage http://www.library.gsu.edu/ and view the Discover field.

You can use Discover for your search, as it searches many other databases. The results, however, are often cumbersome, and many will be irrelevant to your topic.

For a more efficient search, go to the bottom of the Discover search box to click "Databases By Name A-Z." Click "A," and then choose the database "EBSCO Host/Academic Search Complete." You will be asked for your campus ID and password.

Academic Search Complete is a comprehensive, multi-disciplinary source of more than 10,000 scholarly publications. Once you're in Academic Search Complete, conduct a basic search using keywords from your topic (for example, *water quality*), a title, or an author. Academic Search Complete also will limit the results to scholarly journals if you click "Search Options" and then "Scholarly Journals Only." You can also choose to see only articles with full-texts available. You also can earmark desired articles to an electronic folder.

Use Boolean operators to tailor your search. Use quotation marks to search for *phrases*, like "bipolar disorder" or "a midsummer night's dream." Use *AND, OR and NOT*, and make them ALL CAPS, as in biomedical AND engineering NOT nuclear. Use an asterisk* for *wild card searches*; cinema* will return "cinematic" and "cinematography." Use multiple search terms to narrow the results; a search for "environment" will yield millions of hits.

> Note: EBSCO Host/Academic Search Complete is one of more than 100 databases available through the library, serving a wide range of disciplines. For discipline-specific databases, seek out the Subject Librarian for your field (art, for example), or browse "Databases A-Z" in Discover. You'll find everything from NASA's database to MedLine to ARTstor to Rock'N'Roll and Counterculture.

Here are some suggested databases for different disciplines:
- Humanities, including Languages and Literatures—EBSCO Host/Academic Search Complete, JSTOR, MLA International Bibliography, Project Muse
- Social Sciences—ERIC, Government Document Catalog Services, PsychInfo
- Business—ProQuest, LexisNexis Academic
- Sciences—Academic Search Complete, Web of Science, General Science Index
- News, Legal Cases—LexisNexis Academic

Finding Library Books

Scholarly books treat academic topics with in-depth discussion and careful documentation of evidence. They are often published by university presses, such as Oxford University Press or the University of California Press. Sometimes, a well-researched popular book with a thorough bibliography is a good research find; its bibliography can point you toward scholarly books/articles on your topic. Remember: In academic writing, we build on the work of scholars who have come before us.

It is easy to search for library books. Go to the Discover window and click "Catalog"; under "All Fields," search by title, subject, or author. At the bottom of the catalog entry for each book, you will find the location of the book in the Pullen Library:

"Library North 3"—and the call number by which you can find the book on the shelves: "RC516 .B526." Proceed to third floor north and find the RCs on the shelves.

Using Internet Sources Wisely

While conducting research through simply using the Google search bar is inadequate, the World Wide Web can be an incredible resource for legitimate research. Through it, you can find full texts of pending legislation, searchable online editions of Shakespeare's plays, scholarly articles, environmental impact statements, stock quotes, and much more. Finding credible sites for research through a Google search, however, is not that easy. Sites range, in terms of credibility and usefulness, from the spectacularly good (like Google Books, with millions of searchable titles) to the spectacularly bad. When evaluating a web site, it is your job as a scholar to learn to recognize the difference between legitimate resources, and those that are not credible. Remember, you are trying to build ethos: Which is more credible, a paper citing nothing but Web sources? Or, one that uses statistics from published studies, articles from peer-reviewed journals, and news reports providing historical and social context?

A rule of thumb—just like a scholarly journal, a reliable internet source:

1. lists an author,
2. lists its sources, and
3. isn't selling anything.

Researchers, in general, evaluate web sites for *relevance, reliability, accuracy and currency* (as in, how *recent/timely* is the source?) In addition to asking *"How does this information fit my research purpose?"* they ask questions such as:

Who is the author of the site? Is he or she a legitimate expert? What organization or entity does the writer represent? Think of the credibility gap— and the gap between the writer's rhetorical stance and tone—between the American Medical Association website (ama-assn.org) and "The Anti-Liberal Page" (a .com site). Researchers view .com sites, short for "commercial," with a healthy dose of skepticism. The .edu suffix, indicating a college or university, indicates credibility, as does .gov, which indicates a government agency or search engine like www.searchusa.gov.

What is the purpose of the site? What is its agenda? Compare the purpose of a recognized informational website (like the United Nations web site, at http://www.un.org/en/), to the purpose of the www.MartinLutherKing.org. site mentioned earlier. One seeks to provide accurate information; one is a supremacist-group smear campaign that seeks to destroy reputations.

To help you in your Internet research, two specialized search engines yield only results that have been vetted by university librarians for accuracy and credibility. They are:

- Information You Can Trust, http://www.ipl.org, and
- Infomine: Scholarly Internet Resource Collections @ http://infomine. ucr.edu.

THE THESIS STATEMENT AND RESEARCH PROPOSAL

To review, an *argumentative* paper makes an *argument*—a claim—which is supported with specific evidence gleaned from your research.

Early in your research process, your argument—the main claim of your research paper—will begin to take shape, and you will have an idea of how you will use your preliminary sources. In the research proposal, you specify the argument and sources for your research project. The proposal is not a contract, and you are not locked into the topic at this point. In fact, your proposal most likely will be refined, narrowed, or changed based on continual conversation with your instructor and peers, as part of the writing process. As your research proposal develops, think of it as a guide to keep writing and research laser-focused on your thesis.

The art of crafting a research statement (or question) requires study and practice; consult your writing textbook for techniques and examples. As for the research proposal, requirements vary among instructors; they may range from a bare-bones outline (see example below) to a multiple-page written document.

Here is an outline-form proposal with some typical required elements, as assigned by one instructor:

"Colored Bricks of Wisdom" by Nadia Dejou

SAMPLE RESEARCH PROPOSAL

My Classical Argument Proposal: Why Writing Teachers Should Study Depression and Bipolar Disorder in Student Writers

My Audience: Writing teachers, including my writing instructor, and my 1102 class members

My Thesis/Argument: Composition teachers should study how depression and bipolar disorder affect student writing.

Three Reasons Why:

1. Depression and bipolar illness have long been associated with writing creativity.

I knew this, and will find more examples in research.

2. Seven percent of undergraduates nationwide currently take antidepressants; a full one in four say depression has hurt their academic performance.

I knew this generally, but didn't know the numbers until I researched. Wow!

3. Depression can cause writer's block; perhaps not all late papers are due to laziness.

I didn't know this; I found more data to illustrate it.

Possible Counter-Arguments

THEY SAY: Writing teachers don't need to study this. They're not therapists.

I SAY: True, but this affects the writing of many, many students. It's relevant for the study of composition.

Preliminary Research Sources:

At this point, I have found three main source candidates:
1. A website (The National College Health Association's major mental health study of 200 colleges nationwide). *I will use data from this study to illustrate the breadth of depression and bipolar illness in the student population.*
2. An article (from the academic journal *Comprehensive Psychiatry*) *I will use this article for Reason No. 3, that depression can cause writer's block, which may affect students' academic performance.*
3. A library book (published by Columbia University Press) *I will use this book for background on depression and mania in writers in English.*

PLAGIARISM

Before we discuss how to quote, paraphrase, and otherwise work with sources, you should become familiar with the basics of plagiarism.

Intentional plagiarism ranks high in the pantheon of really bad ideas. Its stigma follows students throughout their academic careers. Plagiarism means handing in something you didn't write, and it can be long or short—from an entire paper from an online paper mill to an unattributed catchy phrase. The basic concepts of plagiarism are relatively easy to grasp with a little effort.

At Georgia State, *"The student is responsible for understanding the legitimate use of sources . . . and the consequences of violating this responsibility."* In other words, the burden rests upon you as the writer to give credit where credit is due.

It is in your best interest not to put your instructor in the position of discerning accidental from deliberate plagiarism.

Some very common types of plagiarism
1. Turning in a paper that was written by someone else as your own. This includes papers obtained from online paper mills.
2. Copying from a source without acknowledging that source in the proper format (in English courses, this would be MLA documentation, which

includes a parenthetical citation at the end of the sentence and a source entry on the Works Cited page).

3. Paraphrasing materials from a source without attributing the information to the source.

4. Copying materials from a text but treating them as your own, leaving out quotation marks and acknowledgement.

All instances of plagiarism are reported to the College of Arts & Sciences. Please be sure you understand your instructor's policy for plagiarism as stated on the course syllabus.

GSU students have too many resources to even consider plagiarizing. To learn how to avoid plagiarism and how to properly cite sources, students have not only classroom instruction but also one-on-one conferences with their instructors, tutoring appointments at the GSU Writing Studio, and the availability of comprehensive web sites like The Purdue Online Writing Lab (owl.english.purdue.edu/).

Internet searches, anti-plagiarism software like turnitin.com, and instructors' in-depth knowledge of students' writing make it easy to catch plagiarism among composition students. The "easy way," paradoxically, is simply to do the work.

From the GSU Policy on Academic Honesty (Section 409 of GSU Faculty Handbook)

"The University expects students and faculty to be academically honest, and it expects faculty members to communicate expectations to students in their syllabi. That said, it is the student's final responsibility to understand plagiarism and avoid it. See the definitions below.

GSU's Definitions of Academic Honesty

The examples and definitions given below are intended to clarify the standards by which academic honesty and academically honorable conduct are to be judged. The list is merely illustrative of the kinds of infractions that may occur, and it is not intended to be exhaustive. Moreover, the definitions and examples suggest conditions under which unacceptable behavior of the indicated types normally occurs; however, there may be unusual cases that fall outside these conditions which also will be judged unacceptable by the academic community.

Plagiarism: Plagiarism is presenting another person's work as one's own. Plagiarism includes any paraphrasing or summarizing of the works of another person without acknowledgment, including the submitting of another student's work as one's own. Plagiarism frequently involves a failure to acknowledge in the text, notes, or footnotes the quotation of the paragraphs, sentences, or even a few phrases written or spoken by someone else. The submission of research or completed papers or projects by someone else is plagiarism, as is the unacknowledged use of research sources gathered by someone else when that use is specifically forbidden by the faculty member. Failure to indicate the extent and nature of one's reliance on other sources is also a form of plagiarism. Any work, in whole or in part, taken from the Internet or other computer-based resource without properly referencing the source (for example, the URL) is considered plagiarism. A complete reference is required in order that all parties may locate and view the original source. Finally, there may be forms of plagiarism that are unique to an individual discipline or course, examples of which should be provided in advance by the faculty member. The student is responsible for understanding the legitimate use of sources, the appropriate ways of acknowledging academic, scholarly or creative indebtedness, and the consequences of violating this responsibility.

Cheating on Examinations: Cheating on examinations involves giving or receiving unauthorized help before, during, or after an examination. Examples of unauthorized help include the use of notes, computer based resources, texts, or "crib sheets" during an examination (unless specifically approved by the faculty member), or sharing information with another student during an examination (unless specifically approved by the faculty member). Other examples include intentionally allowing another student to view one's own examination and collaboration before or after an examination if such collaboration is specifically forbidden by the faculty member.

Unauthorized Collaboration: Submission for academic credit of a work product, or a part thereof, represented as its being one's own effort, which has been developed in substantial collaboration with another person or source, or computer-based resource, is a violation of academic honesty. It is also a violation of academic honesty knowingly to provide such assistance. Collaborative work specifically authorized by a faculty member is allowed.

Falsification: It is a violation of academic honesty to misrepresent material or fabricate information in an academic exercise, assignment, or proceeding (e.g., false or misleading citation of sources, the falsification of the results of experiments or of computer data, false or misleading information in an academic context in order to gain an unfair advantage).

Multiple Submissions: It is a violation of academic honesty to submit substantial portions of the same work for credit more than once without the explicit consent of the faculty member(s) to whom the material is submitted for additional credit. In cases in which there is a natural development of research or knowledge in a sequence of courses, use of prior work may be desirable, even required; however the student is responsible for indicating in writing, as a part of such use, that the current work submitted for credit is cumulative in nature."

Two Examples of Plagiarism

Plagiarism takes many forms; two definitive examples follow. Examine the following original passages and student use of them. Determine which one is:

1. Word-for-Word Plagiarism
2. Too-Close Paraphrasing/Lack of Acknowledgement of Sources

Original Passage #1:

"As you read the book, you really do feel for Ender. He's used like a tool, honed and shaped against his will, with no one to turn to, which is pretty much the point. If he's in the midst of battle, there won't be a grownup there to turn to. His childhood is ripped from him, bit by bit, and perhaps that's why you feel sorry for him. By the time the book comes to its climax, he's only eleven years old. He's very smart, and very talented, but he's still only eleven." (From www10brinkster.com/MShades/books/e/ender.html)

A Student's Use #1:

As you read the book, you really do feel for Ender. The idea of a child being used like a tool, having their childhood bypassed and eliminated, is a harsh thing, and perhaps that's the lesson of this book.

Ender is used like a tool, honed and shaped against his will, with no one to turn to. If he's in the midst of battle, there won't be a grownup there to turn to. Ender's childhood is ripped from him, bit by bit, and perhaps that's why you feel sorry for him. By the time the book comes to its climax, he's only eleven years old. He's very smart, but he's still only eleven.

Citation strategies you would use for this example #1:

Review and practice what it means to summarize and/or paraphrase the piece.

Review how to quote the author. Use a page number if available. Here is how: According to Smith, Ender "is used like a tool, honed and shaped against his will" (1).

Use parenthetical citation at the end of sentences both quoted AND paraphrased. If you paraphrase, be sure to introduce the paraphrased material in a way that illustrates the difference between your words and ideas and those you summarize from your source.

Original Passage #2:

"At about 1:01 p.m. on March 18, 1925, trees began to snap north-northwest of Ellington, Missouri, and for the next three and a half hours more people would die, more schools would be destroyed, more students and farmers would be killed, and more deaths would occur in a single city than from any other tornado in U.S. history. Records would be set for speed, path length, and probably for other categories that can't be measured so far in the past. The tornado maintained an exact heading, N 69 degrees E, for 183 of the 219 miles, at an average of 62 mph, following a slight topographic ridge on which a series of mining towns were built. These towns were the main targets of the devastating winds. No distinct funnel was visible through much of its path, yet for over 100 miles, the path width held uniformly at about three-quarters of a mile." (http://www.carolyar.com/Illinois/Misc/Tornado.htm)

A Student's Use #2:

A terrible tornado passed through north-northwest of Ellington, Missouri at about 1:01 p.m. on March 18, 1925. The trees began to snap, and for the next approximately three hours, many people died, many schools were destroyed, and the U.S. record was set for deaths occurring in a single city. Records also would be set for path length and speed. The tornado maintained the heading of N 69 degrees E, and traveled at an average of 62 mph for the length of its path. You couldn't see a funnel, but for more than 100 miles, the monster left a destruction path three-quarters of a mile wide. Big tornadoes like this are the reason that towns and cities should install more tornado warning sirens.

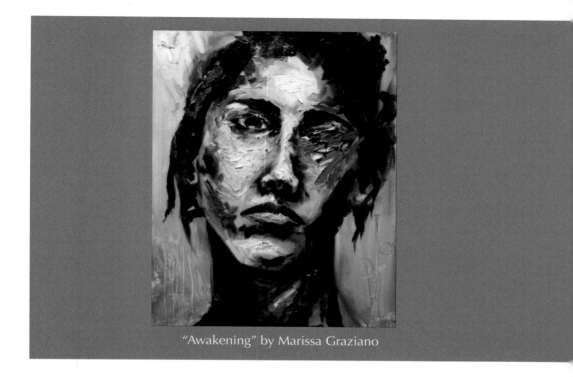

"Awakening" by Marissa Graziano

Determine which is word-for-word plagiarism and which is too-close-paraphrase/didn't cite sources plagiarism. Then, let's revisit the idea of common and uncommon knowledge:

Common Knowledge: Every year, tornadoes kill people in an area of the central U.S. known as Tornado Alley. (You do not have to name a source for this).

***NOT* Common Knowledge:** "The 1925 Missouri tornado maintained an exact heading, N 69 degrees E, at an average of 62 mph." You did not know this as you came into your research. In MLA format, you must name the source of this data, both in 1) parentheses at the end of the sentence, and 2) in the Works Cited page.

In the second example, the student did not *credit a source* when he/she directly quoted and paraphrased facts that are *NOT common knowledge*.

Remember the important rule of thumb: *If a fact wasn't in your head when you began your research, assume it is NOT common knowledge. By the same token, if a fact is new to you but common knowledge to your audience, you may not need to cite it.*

Citation strategies you would use for this example:
*   Put quotation marks around all direct quotes (whole sentences AND phrases).
*   Use a looser, more contextual paraphrase (combine it with text above and below).
*   Use parenthetical citation at the end of fact-laden sentences, both quoted AND paraphrased (Smith 1).

For more on researching and note-taking, understanding plagiarism, and plagiarism examples, consult the "Is It Plagiarism?" and "Safe Practices" sections of the Purdue OWL at http://owl.english.purdue.edu/owl/resource/589/03/. The OWL is an excellent source across the board for research paper writing. These two sections cover reading, note-taking, summarizing, paraphrasing, quoting, and safely writing about the ideas of others.

PLAGIARISM: EASY TO COMMIT, HARD TO LIVE DOWN

In 2006, Harvard undergraduate Kaavya Viswanathan wrote the best-selling novel *How Opal Mehta Got Kissed, Got Wild, and Got A Life*. The novel was subsequently recalled by the publisher—who took the unprecedented step of destroying all copies—because Viswanathan plagiarized throughout.

This is one of many examples of how the writer followed sources much too closely:

From Salman Rushdie's 1990 novel *Haroun and the Sea of Stories*: "If from speed you get your thrill, take precaution, make your will."

From Viswanathan's novel: "If from drink you get your thrill, take precaution—write your will."

TAKING NOTES FROM SOURCES

To "plagiarism-proof" a research paper: As you take notes, ALWAYS indicate which words are YOURS and which are quotes from sources. Find a way that works for you—large quotation marks, highlighting for "mine," etc.

Careful note-taking is the best defense against plagiarism. Note-taking strategies differ among researchers. The purpose of note-taking is to allow you to keep source material organized; it also helps you internalize source material, and makes research writing easier. Whether you're taking notes on paper, on your computer (using a different page or file for each topic), or on a program like Zotero (a Firefox plugin available through the library), be sure to keep neat and organized notes. Here is the basic note card format, for paper, or computer:

Write a subject heading at the top—a category that makes sense to you. Then, carefully enter either 1) *a direct quote of the source, with quote marks* 2) your *summary* of the source, or 3) your *paraphrase* of the source. Write which of the three you have created at the bottom of the card or file.

Google's Data-Gathering Practices (subject heading)

Stallworth, "Googling for Principles in Online Advertising," p. 470

"Google's enormous data-crunching machine is able to make calculated assumptions about consumers based on their searches, or on information consumers reveal when registering for Google's free services."

Direct quote.

Common and Uncommon Knowledge

Once again, to avoid plagiarism, *you must credit a source* when you quote, paraphrase, or summarize *any facts that are not common knowledge* (see below for instructions on how to quote, paraphrase and summarize). For example: "In March of 2012, the population of the United States was estimated at 313,232,882." Or, "The *RMS Titanic* sank on April 15, 1912." Or, "The University of Texas has seven museums and 17 libraries." These facts are not common knowledge, so its source must be cited at the end of the sentence.

You don't have to credit a source for facts that *are* common knowledge: "The United States government is divided into three branches: executive, legislative and judicial." "The University of Texas is in Austin." Depending on context and audience, however, writing "The population of the United States is around 300 million" may be considered common knowledge.

Rule of thumb:

> *If a fact wasn't in your head when you began your research, assume it is NOT common knowledge.*

Preparing Sources for Your Paper

If you've copied words directly from a source without changing them, these copied words must be enclosed in quotation marks. Failure to put quotation marks around copied material is plagiarism, since the reader will believe they are your own words.

Always introduce the quotation with a signal phrase of your own (see below, "For William Styron"), and insert an ellipsis if you take words out of the quote (Use "insert, symbol," in Word, then click on Ellipsis). End the sentence by crediting the source of the quote. Here are the original sentences from William Styron's memoir *Darkness Visible*:

> *(Original) "The madness of depression is, generally speaking, the antithesis of violence. It is a storm indeed, but a storm of murk. Soon evident are the slowed-down responses, near paralysis, psychic energy throttled back close to zero."*

Here is an example, using an ellipsis (...) to mark excised words:

> *(Student Example) For William Styron, the experience of severe depression is "a storm of murk ... of slowed-down responses, near paralysis, psychic energy throttled back to zero" (47).*

Even when you summarize and paraphrase, you still must credit the original author. The preceding example did this in the signal phrase "For William Styron" and by listing the page number in parenthesis at the end of the sentence (47).

IMPORTANT: Never copy words verbatim to your paper unless you use direct, essentially unchanged quotes in quotation marks. Changing only a word or two here or there is plagiarism, and is easy for instructors to catch. To guard against plagiarism, use the following read-think-write strategies.

Direct Quoting of a Source

When using a direct quote, use the source's exact language, and always set off the quote in quotation marks. If you take words out of the source's exact language, always replace them with an ellipsis (...) Always end a quote with a parenthetical citation (often, a page number).

IMPORTANT: Never just drop quotes into your paper. The effect on your audience is jarring, and meaning is often lost. Always use an introductory "signal" verb or phrase.

Examples:

According to Smith, "Quote" (21).

Smith argues that "Quote" (21).

Refer to your writing handbook or a rhetoric text for a list of these "signal" verbs that add smoothness and sophistication to your writing.

Indirect Quoting of a Source (Paraphrasing)

Sometimes, you will want to paraphrase a quote—to put it simply, in your own words, rather than use it verbatim. Paraphrasing is fine as long as you 1) get the source's meaning exactly right and 2) include all the main issues in the order you encounter them in the original sources, and 3) cite the source at the end of the sentence.

Be sure, too, to make it clear where your own thoughts begin and end. Simply putting a parenthetical citation at the end of a paragraph is not sufficient (is the entire paragraph the restating of the source's ideas?). You must introduce the source and discuss the source's relevancy to your topic.

Example:

Job creation is heavy on the minds of the American public. In response to this public concern, at a July 15 press conference, President Obama said he would launch a new job creation program (20). Many of these jobs will be in the environmental and sustainability sector, which means a degree in these two areas will be more advantageous than ever before.

The Rhetorical Précis

The rhetorical précis (pronounced "pray-see") is a highly specialized, brief and useful summary you may be asked to write; writing a précis is an excellent way to summarize sources (as opposed to the simple summary outlined below). It places emphasis on the rhetorical aspects of the work, like author, purpose, and audience. The précis is based on four very specific sentences, which are highlighted in the example below:

1. The first sentence provides the author's name, the genre (article, book), the title, and the date of the work in parentheses. Then, it uses a concise verb (like "claims" or "argues") followed by a "that" phrase stating the thesis of the work. The thesis can be either quoted or paraphrased.
2. The next sentence explains how the author supports his/her thesis. Stay general here; avoid details.
3. The third sentence uses an "in order to" phrase to state the purpose of the piece. Why is the author writing this piece?
4. The last sentence names the author's intended audience.

Durland, Stephen. "Witness: The Guerrilla Theater of Greenpeace." *High Performance* 40 (Winter 1987). *Community Arts Network Reading Room Archives.* Community Arts Network. 1999. 15 February 2009. Web.

In his article "Witness: The Guerrilla Theater of Greenpeace" (1987), writer Stephen Durland argues that the performative environmental rhetoric of Greenpeace should be considered art and should not be overlooked by the world of performance art. In order to make his argument, Durland traces the beginnings of Greenpeace's brand of theater to the "guerrilla theater" of the Yippie movement of Abbie Hoffman and Jerry Rubin in the 1960s, narrates the major symbolic acts of the organization, and interviews Action Director Steve Loper about the group's philosophy and purpose. The purpose of Durland's article is to call attention to the need for an expansion of the sort of activism through art that Greenpeace practices. The audience for Durland's article includes primarily the readers of High Performance, a (now-defunct) magazine for the subgenre of performance art.

Taking Notes: Summarizing a Source

A *summary*, as opposed to a précis, simply condenses the original material, presenting its core ideas *in your own words*. Use it to condense long passages that emphasize your point, and when details are not critical. Don't use "I," or evaluate the piece. Just condense.

1. In the first sentence, state the article's main claim, or thesis; begin with the author's full name, the title of the article (in quotation marks), and page numbers.
2. State the major supporting points in their original order. Omit details and examples.
3. End with the author's conclusions or recommendations.

Taking Notes: Paraphrasing a Source

A *paraphrase*, on the other hand, reflects *your* understanding of the source. A paraphrase includes *all* points and ideas in the same order as originally written by the author. You should use the paraphrase when direct quoting is not permitted. Paraphrasing represents a by-product of your learning process, and as such communicates the ideas in your own words without condensing the material. Use your own language and structure. That being said, paraphrasing is a tricky process. In writing, you should always aim to differentiate your ideas from those ideas published by others. You can see how paraphrasing might lead you to inadvertently pass off someone's ideas as your own.

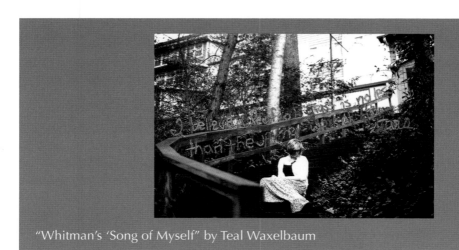

"Whitman's 'Song of Myself'" by Teal Waxelbaum

Rule of Thumb:

> *If you are using information to support a claim you make in your paper, it is best to use direct quotes. If you paraphrase, remember you must indicate (in writing) where your thoughts begin and end. So, even paraphrased material must be introduced and explained by your own writing. And, of course, paraphrased ideas must be properly cited.*

Paraphrasing with The Look-Away Method—Read one or two sentences over several times. Then set the article aside and paraphrase the meaning of the sentences without looking back at the article. When you are finished, review the article and make sure your paraphrase is accurate and that you didn't actually quote it.

Consider this original text from page 141 of Nicholas Carr's *The Shallows: What the Internet is Doing To Our Brains* (2010):

Original: "Given our brain's plasticity, we know that our online habits continue to reverberate in the workings of our synapses when we're not online. We can assume that the neural circuits devoted to scanning, skimming, and multitasking are expanding and strengthening, while those used for reading and thinking deeply, with sustained concentration, are weakening or eroding. In 2009, researchers from Stanford University found signs that this shift may already be well underway. They gave a battery of cognitive tests to a group of heavy media multitaskers as well as a group of relatively light multitaskers. They found that the heavy multitaskers were much more easily distracted by "irrelevant environmental stimuli," had less control over the contents of their working memory, and were in general much less able to maintain their concentration on a particular task."

Student Paraphrase: Carr makes the assumption that heavy use of brain pathways involved in scanning and skimming information online has a strengthening effect on those circuits, while pathways used for deep reading and concentration atrophy. He cites a 2009 Stanford study suggesting that multitaskers were more distractable and less in control of memory and concentration (141).

Note: For each summary or paraphrase, always record the relevant page numbers for the article in parentheses. This will save you a great deal of hunting and work toward the end of your paper, when you prepare the Works Cited list.

Taking Notes: The Annotated Bibliography

At some point in the research project, you may be asked to create an Annotated Bibliography. For each entry, you annotate the source (write a brief summary or paraphrase), and include a few sentences on how the source is relevant to your research project. An annotated bibliography, written as you research, is an ideal reference for you to use as your prepare your final paper. Here is a sample annotation:

Ehrenreich, Barbara. "Nickel and Dimed." *Mothering*. 2001. *Academic Search Complete*. Web. 10 May 2011.

> *In this article, Ehrenreich discusses welfare assistance in America as it applies to single parents, as well as how minimum wage affects these households. She argues against the idea that putting single mothers on welfare increases the likelihood that they will keep having children they cannot take care of. She uses statistics to prove that most people who go on welfare are hardworking individuals who just do not make enough on their own to support themselves, much less their children. This article will help me to show that while the government does offer assistance to single parents, it does not offer enough, and it offers assistance in a way that makes the general public scoff at and belittle those who accept it. This also will help me highlight what individuals who received welfare really do with the money, to build the credibility of hardworking single parents who do not abuse the system.*

MLA Documentation

When you do research to find supporting evidence for your ideas or arguments, you need to credit your outside sources. Depending on what type of essay you are writing or which type of course you are writing for, you will need to choose a documentation style and continue with that style for the entire essay. Two of the most common styles, especially for freshman and sophomore students, are MLA (Modern Language Association) and APA (American Psychological Association).

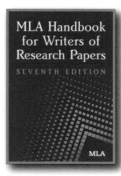

If you write in composition, language, linguistics, and literature courses, you will often be asked to use documentation guidelines created by the Modern Language Association (MLA). The *MLA Handbook for Writers of Research Papers*, in its seventh edition, provides a full description of the conventions used by this particular community of writers; updates to the *MLA Handbook* can be found at <www.mla.org>.

MLA guidelines require that you give both an in-text citation and a Works Cited entry for any and all sources you use. Using accurate in-text citations helps guide your reader to the appropriate entry on the Works Cited. For example, the in-text citation given below in parentheses directs the reader to the correct page of the book given in the Works Cited.

> In-text citation➔When a teenager sleeps more than 10 hours per night, it is time to question whether she is having significant problems (Jones 63).

Entry in Works Cited➜
Jones, Stephanie. *The Signs of Trouble*. Boston: Dilemma

Publishing, 2010. Print.

This chapter provides a general overview of MLA documentation style and an explanation of the most commonly used MLA documentation formats, including a few significant revisions since the previous edition.

Did You Know?

The Modern Language Association was founded in 1883 at The John Hopkins University as a group that discussed literature and modern languages, such as Spanish, French, Chinese, and English. The MLA, now with over 30,000 members in over 100 countries, is the primary professional association for literature and language scholars.

37a Using MLA in-text citations

In-text citations (also called *parenthetical citations*) point readers to where they can find more information about your researched supporting materials. When you use MLA documentation style, you need to indicate the author's last name and the location of the source material (page or paragraph number). Where this in-text information is placed depends on how you want to phrase the sentence that is summarized, paraphrased, or quoted. Be sure that the in-text citation guides the reader clearly to the source in the Works Cited, where complete information about the source is given.

The following are some of the most common examples of parenthetical citations.

1. Author's name in text

When using a parenthetical reference to a single source that is already named in the sentence, use this form: (Page number). Note that the period goes after the parentheses.

→ Stephanie Jones, author of *The Signs of Trouble*, describes "excessive sleeping, refraining from eating, and lying about simple things" as signs to look for when parents are concerned about their children (63).

2. Author's name in reference

When the author's name is not included in the preceding sentence, use this form for the parenthetical information at the end of the sentence: (Author's Last Name Page number). Note that there is no comma between the name and page in an MLA parenthetical reference, and also note that the period comes at the end of the sentence after the parentheses.

→ When a teenager sleeps more than 10 hours per night, it is time to question whether she is having significant problems (Jones 63).

3. No author given

When a work has no credited author, use a clipped version of the work's title.

→ In a recent *Time* article, a list of 30 common signs of teenage trouble cites lack of sleep as the most common sign ("Thirty" 3).

4. Two or three authors given

When you use a source that was written by two or three authors, use all the names in the text of the sentence or in the citation.

→ The idea that "complexity is a constant in biology" is not an innovative one (Sole and Goodwin 2).

→ Most signs in English that the authors encountered on the road had "grammar mistakes, misspellings, or just odd pictures" (Smith, Jones, and Best 55).

5. Four or more authors given

MLA documentation style allows a choice when there are four authors or more of an item to be cited. You can either name all the authors or include only the first author's name followed by *et al.* (Latin for "and others").

→ In Hong Kong, most signs are in Chinese and English; however, once you are in mainland China, English is rarely found on signs, except in tourist areas (Li, Smith, Jones, and Franz 49).

→ In Hong Kong, most signs are in Chinese and English; however, once you are in mainland China, English is rarely found on signs, except in tourist areas (Li, et al. 49).

6. Authors with the same last names

If your source material includes items by authors who happen to have the same last name, be sure to use each author's first name or initial in the parentheses.

→ When a teenager sleeps more than 10 hours per night, it is time to question whether she is having significant problems (S. Jones 63).

→ Another sign of trouble can be when you do not see your child for meals (B. Jones 114).

7. Encyclopedia or dictionary unsigned entry

When you use an encyclopedia or dictionary to look up a word or entry, be sure to include the word or entry title in the parenthetical entry.

→ The word *thing* has more definitions than any other entry in the *Oxford English Dictionary* ("thing").

8. Lines of verse (plays, poetry or song lyrics)

For plays, give the act, scene, and line numbers that are located in any edition of the play. Separate the act, scene, and line numbers with periods. For example, the quotation below comes from *Romeo and Juliet*, Act II, Scene 2, lines 43 and 44. The MLA also advises using this method with biblical chapters and verses. Be sure, though, that the sequence goes from largest unit to smallest unit.

→ Juliet grapples with how names can influence feelings as she questions, "What's in a name? That which we call a rose/By any other name would smell as sweet" (2.2.43-44).

Use a slash (/) to signify line breaks when you quote poetry or song lyrics, and put line numbers in the in-text citation instead of page numbers.

→ An early song by Will Smith shows the frustration of children as he sings, "You know parents are the same/No matter time nor place/They don't understand that us kids/Are going to make some mistakes" (1-4).

9. Indirect quotation

When you use a quotation of a quotation—that is, a quotation that quotes from another source—use *qtd. in* to designate the source.

→ Smith has said, "My parents really didn't understand me" (qtd. in Jones, par. 8).

37b Using long or block quotations

Long or block quotations have special formatting requirements of their own.

1. Block quote of prose

If you quote a chunk of prose that is longer than four typed lines, you are using what is called a *block quotation*. Follow these MLA guidelines for block quotations:

1. If introducing the block quotation with a sentence, use a colon at the end of the sentence.

2. Begin the quotation on a new line.

3. Do not use quotation marks to enclose the block quote.

4. Indent the quote one inch from the left margin, and extend the right margin to the end of the line.

5. Double space the entire quotation.

6. Put a period at the end of the quotation, and then add the parenthetical citation.

→ However, Lansky states:

> Despite the statement on <www.signspotting.com> that we don't accept signs with the intention of being funny, people like sending them in. I've opted not to use these as it could encourage people to start making them, sticking them up in their driveway, and snapping a picture. Plus, funny signs are so much more amusing when the humor is accidental. (72)

2. Block quote of poetry, drama, or song lyrics

For songs and poems, be sure to give line numbers rather than page numbers and to use the original line breaks.

→ The Fresh Prince, an early Will Smith character, sings about parents not understanding:

> You know parents are the same
> No matter time or place
> They don't understand that us kids
> Are going to make some mistakes
> So to you other kids all across the land
> There's no need to argue
> Parents just don't understand. (4-7)

37c   Adding or omitting words in a quotation

1. Adding words to a quotation

Use square brackets ([ ]) to point out words or phrases that are not part of the original text.

→ Original quotation: "When we entered the People's Republic of China, we noticed that the signage began dropping English translations."

→ Quotation with added word: She said, "When we entered the People's Republic of China, [Dunkirk and I] noticed that the signage began dropping English translations" (Donelson 141).

You can also add your own comments inside a quotation by using square brackets. For example, you can add the word *sic* to a quotation when you know that there is an error.

→ Original quotation: "When we entered the People's Repulic of China, we noticed that the signage began dropping English translations."

→ Quotation with added comment: She said, "When we entered the People's Repulic [sic] of China, we noticed that the signage began dropping English translations" (Donelson 141).

2. Omitting words in a quotation

Use an ellipsis (. . .) to represent words that you delete from a quotation. The ellipsis begins with a space, then has three periods with spaces between them, and then ends with a space.

Original quotation→ "The Great Wall is something that can be seen from space. When we reach a time when advertisements can be seen from space, we have probably gone too far."

Quotation with words omitted in middle of sentence➜ Frank Donelson, author of *Signs in Space*, remarks, "The Great Wall . . . can be seen from space. When we reach a time when advertisements can be seen from space, we have probably gone too far" (178).

If you omit words at the end of a quotation, and that is also the end of your sentence, use an ellipsis plus a period with no space before the ellipsis or after the period.

Original quotation➜ "The Great Wall is something that can be seen from space. When we reach a time when advertisements can be seen from space, we have probably gone too far with our advertising and signage."

Quotation with words omitted at end of sentence➜ Frank Donelson, author of *Signs in Space*, remarks, "The Great Wall is something that can be seen from space. When we reach a time when advertisements can be seen from space, we have probably gone too far. . ." (178).

> **Helpful hint**
>
> MLA guidelines can change with a new edition. Sometimes, class textbooks can use an older MLA documentation style. Always check with your instructor if rules seem to be in conflict.

37d Citing online sources

In the MLA documentation style, online or electronic sources have their own formatting guidelines since these types of sources rarely give specific page numbers.

The MLA recommends that you include in the text, rather than in an in-text citation, the name(s) of the person (e.g., author, editor, director, performer) that begins the matching Works Cited entry. For instance, the following is the recommended way to begin an in-text citation for an online source:

➔ Roger Ebert says that Shyamalan "plays the audience like a piano" in the film *Signs* (par. 8).

If the author or creator of the Web site uses paragraph or page numbers, use these numbers in the parenthetical citation. If no numbering is used, do not use or add numbers to the paragraphs, pages, or parenthetical citation.

When Web site does not number paragraphs➔ In his review of the film *Signs*, Roger Ebert says that Shyamalan "does what Hitchcock said he wanted to do, and plays the audience like a piano."

When Web site numbers paragraphs➔ In his review of the film *Signs*, Roger Ebert says that Shyamalan "does what Hitchcock said he wanted to do, and plays the audience like a piano" (par. 8).

37e General formatting guidelines for the MLA Works Cited

If you cite any sources within a paper, be sure to include a Works Cited at the end of the paper. Here are some general formatting guidelines to follow when setting up a Works Cited.

1. Put the Works Cited at the end of your paper as a separate page.

2. Use one-inch margins on all sides.

3. Include any header used for the paper on the Works Cited.

4. Center the title Works Cited at the top of the page, using no underlining, quotation marks, or italics.

5. Place the first line of each entry flush left with the margin. Indent any additional lines of the entry one-half inch (or one tab).

6. Double space the entries in the Works Cited, not adding any extra spaces between entries.

7. Alphabetize the Works Cited. Use the first major word in each entry, not including articles such as *a*, *an*, or *the*, to determine the alphabetical order. If the cited source does not have an author, alphabetize by using the first word of the title of the source.

8. Put author's last name first (e.g., Ebert, Roger). Only reverse the first author's name. If more than one author, follow the first author's name with a comma, and add the other author names in the order of first then last names (e.g., Ebert, Roger, and Gene Siskel).

9. Use hyphens when you use more than one source from the same author. Alphabetize the titles, use the author's full name for the first entry, and then use three hyphens to replace the author's name in all entries after the first (see 37f3).

10. Capitalize all words in titles except for articles, conjunctions, and short prepositions. Always capitalize the first word of a subtitle.

11. Use quotation marks for titles of shorter works, including articles, book chapters, episodes on television or radio, poems, and short stories.

12. Italicize the titles of longer works, including album or CD titles, art pieces, books, films, journals, magazines, newspapers, and television shows.

13. Give the edition number for works with more than one edition (e.g., *MLA Handbook for Writers of Research Papers*, 7th edition).

14. Use the word *Print* after print sources and *Web* for Internet or Web sources.

37f Formats for print sources

1. Books (includes brochures, pamphlets, and graphic novels)

Author's Name. *Title of Book*. Place of publication: Publisher, date of publication. Print.

➔ Lansky, Doug. *Signspotting*. Oakland, CA: Lonely Planet, 2005. Print.

Helpful hint

Only use the state after the city if the city is not a place that would be commonly known or if there may be more than one commonly known city by that name.

2. Books with two or more authors

A comma is used between the author names, even if there are only two authors.

First Author's Name, and second Author's Name. *Title of Book*. Place of publication: Publisher, date of publication. Print.

➔ Maasik, Sonia, and Jack Soloman. *Signs of Life in the USA: Readings on Popular Culture for Writers.* 6th edition. Boston: Bedford/St. Martin's, 2008. Print.

3. Two books by the same author

Use three hyphens and a period in place of the author name(s) in the consecutive entries. Be sure the entries are in alphabetical order.

➔ Maasik, Sonia, and Jack Soloman. *California Dreams and Realities: Readings for Critical Thinkers and Writers.* 3rd edition. Boston: Bedford/St. Martin's, 2004. Print.

➔ ---. *Signs of Life in the USA: Readings on Popular Culture for Writers.* 6th edition. Boston: Bedford/St. Martin's, 2008. Print.

4. Anthology or collection

Editor's Name(s), ed. *Title of Book*. Place of publication: Publisher, date. Print.

➔ Smith, Allison D., Trixie G. Smith, and Karen Wright, eds. *COMPbiblio: Leaders and Influences in Composition Theory and Practice.* Southlake, TX: Fountainhead Press, 2007. Print.

5. Work within an anthology

Author's Name. "Title of Work." *Title of Anthology*. Ed. Editor's Name(s). Place of publication: Publisher, date. Pages. Print.

➔ Tan, Amy. "Mother Tongue." *The Norton Field Guide to Writing*. Ed. Richard Bullock, et al. New York: Norton, 2010. 564-70. Print.

6. Article in a scholarly journal

Author's Name. "Title of the Article." *Journal Title* vol. number (date of publication): pages. Print.

➔ Holbrook, Teri. "An Ability Traitor at Work: A Treasonous Call to Subvert Writing from Within." *Qualitative Inquiry* 16.3 (2010): 171-83. Print.

7. Article in a scholarly journal that uses only issue numbers

Author's Name. "Title of the Article." *Journal Title* issue number (date of publication): pages. Print.

➔ Franks, Lola. "The Play in Language." *Child Signs* 73 (2006): 3-17. Print.

8. Article in a newspaper

Author's Name. "Title of Article." *Newspaper Title* Day Month Year: pages. Print.

➔ Genzlinger, Neil. "Autism is Another Thing that Families Share." *New York Times* 6 Apr. 2010: A4. Print.

Note: when citing English language newspapers, use the name on the masthead but be sure to omit any introductory article (*New York Times*, not *The New York Times*).

9. Article in a magazine

Author's Name. "Title of Article." *Magazine Title* Day Month Year: pages. Print.

Note: only use day if magazine is published on a weekly or bi-weekly basis.

> → Musico, Christopher. "Sign 'Em Up!" *CRM Magazine* Nov. 2009: 49. Print.

10. Review

Reviewer's Name. "Title of Review." Rev. of *Title of Work*, by name of author (editor, director, etc.). *Journal or Newspaper Title* Day Month Year: pages. Print.

> → Ebert, Roger. "A Monosyllabic Superhero Who Wouldn't Pass the Turing Test." Rev. of *X-Men Origins: Wolverine*, by Dir. Gavin Hood. *Chicago Sun-Times* 29 Apr. 2009: E4. Print.

11. Article in a reference book

Author's Name. "Title of Article." *Title of Reference Book*. Ed. Editor's Name. Location: Publisher, date. Pages. Print.

> → Jones, Amber. "Semiotics." *Encyclopedia of Signs*. Ed. Jeffrey Haines and Maria Smith. Boston: Brown, 2003. 199-202. Print.

12. Religious works

Title of Work. Ed. Editor's Name. Place of publication: Publisher, date. Print.

> → *Zondervan NIV Study Bible*. Fully rev. ed. Ed. Kenneth L. Barker. Grand Rapids, MI: Zondervan, 2002. Print.

| 37g | **Formats for online sources** |

Helpful hint

Including the URL is optional under the 7th edition of the *MLA Handbook for Writers of Research Papers*, so only include it after the "Date of Access" **in angle brackets** (<, >) if your source cannot be easily found by typing the author and title into a search engine or if your professor requires it.

1. Web site

Author's Name (if author given). *Name of Page.* Name of institution or organization associated with the Web site. Date of posting/revision. Web. Date of access.

➔ *Services Locator.* United States Post Office. 2010. Web. 9 Feb. 2010.

2. Article on a Web site (including blogs and wikis)

Author's Name. "Article Title." *Name of Web site.* Name of institution or organization associated with the Web site. Date of posting/ revision. Web. Date of access.

Note: If there is no author given, begin the citation with the article title.

➔ "China's Traditional Dress: Qipao." *China Today.* Oct. 2001. Web. 9 Feb. 2010.

➔ Ebert, Roger. "Signs." *rogerebert.com Movie Reviews. Chicago Sun-Times.* 2 Aug. 2002. Web. 9 Feb. 2010.

3. Online newspaper or magazine

Author's Name. "Title of Article." *Newspaper Title* Day Month Year: pages. Web. Date of access.

➔ Bailey, Holly. "The Sign of the Red Truck." *Newsweek* 2007: 1. Web. 9 Feb. 2010.

4. Online journal article

> **Helpful hint**
>
> If the online journal does not include page numbers, use *n. pag.* to indicate this.

Author's Name. "Title of Article." *Title of Journal* Vol. Issue (Year): pages. Web. Date of access.

→ Austen, Veronica. "Writing Spaces: Performances of the Word." *Kairos* 8.1 (2003): n. pag. Web. 9 Feb. 2010.

5. Article from an online service, such as General One-File or LexisNexis

Author's Name. "Title of the Article." *Journal Title* vol. issue (Date of publication): pages. Name of database or other relevant information. Access Provider. Web. Date of access.

Franks, Elizabeth. "Signing Up for Trouble." *Semiotics and Signs* 13.4 (2009): 112-7. *InfoTrac OneFile*. Thomson Gale. Middle Tennessee State University. Web. 9 Feb. 2010.

6. Article from an online reference work

Author's (or editor's) Name. "Title of Article." *Title of Reference Work.* Location, Date of publication (Day Month Year). Web. Date of access (Day Month Year).

Jones, Amber. "Semiotics." *Encyclopedia of Signs.* U of AK, 20 Mar. 2009. Web. 21 Sept. 2010.

37h Formats for other commonly used sources

1. Television or radio program

"Title of Episode or Segment." *Title of Program or Series.* Name of network. Call letters and city of the local station (if applicable). Broadcast date. Medium of reception (e.g., Radio, Television). Supplemental information (e.g., Transcript).

➔ "Signs and Wonders." *The X Files.* FOX. 23 Jan. 2000. Television.

2. Sound recording

Artist/Band. "Song Title." *Title of Album.* Manufacturer, year of issue. Medium (e.g., Audiocassette, CD, Audiotape, LP, Digital download).

➔ Five Man Electrical Band. "Signs." *Good-byes and Butterflies.* Lionel Records, 1970. LP.

➔ Tesla. "Signs." *Five Man Acoustical Jam.* Geffen, 1990. CD.

3. Film

Title. Dir. Director's Name. Perf. Actor's Name(s) (if relevant). Distributor, year of release. Medium.

➔ *Signs.* Dir. M. Night Shyamalan. Perf. Mel Gibson. Touchstone, 2002. Film.

You may also include other information about the film, such as the names of the writers, performers, and producers, after the director's name.

➔ *Signs.* Dir. M. Night Shyamalan. Perf. Mel Gibson. Ex. Prod. Kathleen Kennedy. Touchstone, 2002. Film.

If you would like to highlight the specific contribution of one actor, director, or writer, you may begin the entry with that person's name, as you do with an author for a book.

> ➔ Phoenix, Joaquin, perf. *Signs*. Dir. M. Night Shyamalan. Touchstone, 2002. Film.

4. Advertisement

Name of product, company, or institution. Advertisement. Publisher date of publication. Medium of publication.

> ➔ SunChips. Advertisement. *Newsweek* 15 Jan. 2010: 33. Print.

> ➔ SunChips. Advertisement. NBC. 15 Jan. 2010. Television.

Note the difference in how the citations for print and television advertisements are formatted.

5. Painting, sculpture, or photograph

Artist's Name. *Title*. Creation date (if known). Medium of Composition. Name of institution that houses the work or the individual who owns the work, City.

> ➔ da Vinci, Leonardo. *Mona Lisa*. c. 1503-6. Oil on Poplar. Louvre, Paris.

6. Interview

Interviewee's Name. Descriptive Title of Interview (e.g., Personal, Telephone, Webcam). Date of interview.

> ➔ Elbow, Peter. Personal Interview. 1 Jan. 2009.

7. Lecture, speech, address, or reading

Author's Name. "Title of Speech." Relevant information of where
speech was given. Date of presentation. Descriptive label (e.g.,
Lecture, Speech, Address, Reading).

→ Stephens, Liberty. "The Signs of the Times." MLA
Annual Convention. Hilton Downtown, New York.
28 Dec. 2009. Address.

37i **Sample Works Cited using MLA**

Following is an example of how a completed Works Cited would look
at the end of your paper.

Your Last name   14

Works Cited

Ebert, Roger. "Signs." *rogerebert.com Movie Reviews. Chicago*

Sun-Times. 2 Aug. 2002. Web. 9 Feb. 2010.

Five Man Electrical Band. "Signs." *Good-byes and Butterflies.*

Lionel Records, 1970. LP.

Signs. Dir. M. Night Shyamalan. Perf. Mel Gibson. Touchstone,

2002. Film.

Stephens, Liberty. "The Signs of the Times." MLA Annual

Convention. Hilton Downtown, New York. 28 Dec. 2009.

Address.

APA Documentation

When you do research to find supporting evidence for your ideas or arguments, you need to credit your outside sources. Depending on what type of essay you are writing or which type of course you are writing for, you will need to choose a type of documentation style and continue with that style for the entire essay. Two of the most common styles, especially for freshman and sophomore students, are MLA (Modern Language Association) and APA (American Psychological Association).

If you write an essay in the social sciences, you will usually be asked to use documentation guidelines created by the American Psychological Association. The *Publication Manual of the American Psychological Association*, in its sixth edition, provides a full description of the conventions used by this particular community of writers; updates to the APA manual can be found at <www.apastyle.org>.

Did You Know?

The American Psychological Association was founded in 1892 at Clark University. The APA, now with over 152,000 members, is the primary professional association for social science scholars in the United States.

This chapter provides a general overview of APA documentation style and an explanation of the most commonly used APA documentation formats.

38a   Using APA in-text citations

In-text citations (also called *parenthetical citations*) point readers to where they can find more information about your researched supporting materials. In APA documentation style, the author's last name (or the title of the work, if no author is listed) and the date of publication must appear in the body text of your paper. The author's name can appear either in the sentence itself or in parentheses following the quotation or paraphrase. The date of publication can appear either in the sentence itself, surrounded by parentheses, or in the parentheses that follow the quotation or paraphrase. The page number(s) always appears in the parentheses following a quotation or close paraphrase.

Your parenthetical citation should give enough information to identify the source that was used for the research material as the same source that is listed in your References list. Where this in-text information is placed depends on how you want to phrase the sentence that is summarized, paraphrased, or quoted. Be sure that the in-text citation guides the reader clearly to the source in the References list, where complete information about the source is given.

The following are some of the most common examples of in-text citations.

1. Author's name and date in reference

When using a parenthetical reference to a single source by a single author, use this form: (Author's Last name, Year of publication). Note that the period is placed after the parenthetical element ends.

→   When a teenager sleeps more than 10 hours per night, it is time to question whether she is having significant problems (Jones, 1999).

2. Author's name and date in text

In APA, you can also give the author's name and date within the sentence, using this form: Author's Full Name (Year of publication)

➔ Stephanie Jones (1999) describes the signs to look for and when to be concerned.

3. Using a partial quotation in text

When you cite a specific part of a source, give the page number, using *p.* (for one page) and *pp.* (for two or more pages).

➔ Stephanie Jones (1999) describes the signs parents should look for when concerned about their children: "excessive sleeping, refraining from eating, and lying about simple things" (p. 63).

4. No author given

When a work has no credited author, use the first two or three words of the work's title or the name that begins the entry in the References list. The title of an article or chapter should be in quotation marks, and the title of a book or periodical should be in italics. Inside the parenthetical citation, place a comma between the title and year.

➔ In a recent *Time* article, a list of 30 common signs of teenage trouble cites lack of sleep as the most common sign ("Thirty," 2010).

5. Two to five authors given

When you use a source that was written by two to five authors, you must use all the names in the citation. For the in-text citation, when a work has two authors, use both names each time the reference occurs in the text. When a work has three to five authors, give all authors the first time the reference occurs in the text, and then, in subsequent citations, use only the surname of the first author followed by *et al.* (Latin for "and others") and the year for the first citation of the reference in a paragraph.

→ The idea that "complexity is a constant in biology" is not an innovative one (Sole & Goodwin, 1997, p. 63).

The last two authors' names in a string of three to five authors are separated by a comma and an ampersand (e.g., Jones, Smith, Black, & White).

→ Most signs in English that the authors encountered on the road had "grammar mistakes, misspellings, or just odd pictures" (Smith, Jones, & Best, 1999, p. 55). The most common mistake was an "incorrect or misplaced apostrophe" (Smith, et al., p. 56).

6. Six or more authors given

When there are six authors or more of an item to be cited, include only the first author's name followed by *et al.* (Latin for "and others"). Use this form for the first reference of this text and all references of this text after that. Note: be sure, though, to list all six or more of the authors in your References list.

→ In Hong Kong, most signs are in Chinese and English; however, once you are in mainland China, English is rarely found on signs, except in tourist areas (Li, et al., 2007).

7. Authors with the same last names

If your source material includes items by authors who happen to have the same last name, be sure to use each author's initials in all text citations.

→ When a teenager sleeps more than 10 hours per night, it is time to question whether she is having significant problems (S. Jones, 1999, p. 63).

→ Another sign of trouble can be when you do not see your child for meals (B. Jones, 2003, p. 114).

8. Encyclopedia or dictionary unsigned entry

When you use an encyclopedia or dictionary to look up a word or entry, be sure to include the word or entry title in the parenthetical entry.

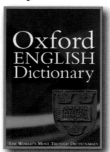

→ The word *thing* has more definitions than any other entry in the *Oxford English Dictionary* ("thing," 2001).

9. Indirect quotation

When you use a quotation of a quotation—that is, a quotation that quotes from another source—use "as cited in" to designate the secondary source.

→ Smith has said, "My parents really didn't understand me" (as cited in Jones, 1990, p. 64).

10. Personal communication

Personal communications—private letters, memos, non-archived emails, interviews—are usually considered unrecoverable information and, as such, are not included in the References list. However, you do include them in parenthetical form in the text, giving the initials and surname of the communicator and providing as exact a date as possible.

→ A. D. Smith (personal communication, February 2, 2010)

→ J. Elbow (personal interview, January 6, 2009)

38b   Using long or block quotations

Long or block quotations have special formatting requirements of their own. If your quotation is prose and longer than 40 words, this is called a *block quotation*. Follow these APA guidelines for block quotations.

1. If introducing the block quotation with a sentence, use a colon at the end of the sentence.

2. Begin the quotation on a new line.

3. Do not use quotation marks to enclose the block quote.

4. Indent the quote five spaces from the left margin, and extend the right margin to the end of the line.

5. Double space the entire quotation.

6. Indent the first line of any additional paragraph.

7. Put a period at the end of the quotation, and then add the parenthetical citation.

→ However, Lansky (1999) states:

> Despite the statement on <www.signspotting.com> that we don't accept signs with the intention of being funny, people like sending them in. I've opted not to use these as it could encourage people to start making them, sticking them up in their driveway, and snapping a picture. Plus, funny signs are so much more amusing when the humor is accidental. (p. 72)

38c — Adding or omitting words in a quotation

1. Adding words in a quotation

Use square brackets ([ ]) to point out words or phrases that are not part of the original text.

→ Original quotation: "When we entered the People's Republic of China, we noticed that the signage began dropping English translations" (Donelson, 2001, p. 141).

→ Quotation with added word: She said, "When we entered the People's Republic of China, [Dunkirk and I] noticed that the signage began dropping English translations" (Donelson, 2001, p. 141).

You can also add your own comments inside a quotation by using square brackets. For example, you can add the word *sic* to a quotation when you know that there is an error.

→ Original quotation: "When we entered the People's Repulic of China, we noticed that the signage began dropping English translations" (Donelson, 2001, p. 141).

➔ Quotation with added comment: She said, "When we entered the People's Repulic [sic] of China, we noticed that the signage began dropping English translations" (Donelson, 2001, p. 141).

2. Omitting words in a quotation

Use an ellipsis (. . .) to represent words that you delete from a quotation. The ellipsis begins with a space, then has three periods with spaces between them, and then ends with a space.

> Original quotation➔ "The Great Wall is something that can be seen from space. When we reach a time when advertisements can be seen from space, we have probably gone too far" (Jones, 1993, p. 101).

> Quotation with words omitted in middle of sentence➔ Frank Jones, author of *Signs in Space*, remarks, "The Great Wall . . . can be seen from space. When we reach a time when advertisements can be seen from space, we have probably gone too far" (1993, p. 101).

If you omit words at the end of a quotation, and that is also the end of your sentence, you should use an ellipsis plus a period with no space before the ellipsis or after the period. Only use an ellipsis if words have been omitted.

> Original quotation➔ "The Great Wall is something that can be seen from space. When we reach a time when advertisements can be seen from space, we have probably gone too far with our advertising and signage" (Jones, 1993, p. 45).

> Quotation with words omitted at end of sentence➔ Frank Jones, author of *Signs in Space*, remarks, "The Great Wall is something that can be seen from space. When we reach a time when advertisements can be seen from space, we have probably gone too far . . ." (1993, p. 45).

Helpful hint

APA guidelines can change with a new edition. Sometimes, class textbooks can use an older APA documentation style. Always check with your instructor if rules seem to be in conflict.

38d Citing online sources

In the APA documentation style, online or electronic sources have their own formatting guidelines since these types of sources rarely give specific page numbers.

The APA recommends that you include in the text, rather than in an in-text citation, the name(s) of the person that begins the matching References list entry. If the author or creator of the Web site uses paragraph or page numbers, use these numbers in the parenthetical citation. If no numbering is used, do not use or add numbers to the paragraphs, pages, or parenthetical citation.

When Web site does not number paragraphs➜ In his review of the film *Signs*, Roger Ebert says that Shyamalan "does what Hitchcock said he wanted to do, and plays the audience like a piano."

When Web site numbers paragraphs➜ In his review of the file *Signs*, Roger Ebert says that Shyamalan "does what Hitchcock said he wanted to do, and plays the audience like a piano" (para. 8).

38e General formatting guidelines for the APA References list

If you cite any sources within a paper, be sure to include a References list at the end of the paper. Here are some general formatting guidelines to follow when setting up a References list.

1. Put the References list at the end of your paper as a separate page.

2. Use one-inch margins on all sides.

3. Include any header used for the paper on the References page.

4. Center the title **References** at the top of the page, using no underlining, quotation marks, or italics.

5. Place the first line of each entry flush left with the margin. Indent any additional lines of the entry one-half inch (or one tab) to form a hanging indent.

6. Double space the entries in the References list, not adding any extra spaces between entries.

7. Alphabetize the References list. Use the first major word in each entry, not including articles such as *a, an,* or *the,* to determine the alphabetical order. If the cited source does not have an author, alphabetize by using the first word of the title of the source.

8. Put author's last name first and then the initial representing the author's first name and the initial for the author's middle name, if given (e.g., Ebert, R.). If a work has more than one author, invert all the authors' names, follow each with a comma, and then continue listing all the authors, putting a comma and ampersand (,&) before the final name (e.g., Ebert, R., & Siskel, G.).

9. Arrange two or more works by the same author(s) in the same name order by year of publication.

10. Capitalize only the first word in a title and a subtitle unless the title or subtitle includes a proper noun, which would also be capitalized.

11. Do not use quotation marks for titles of shorter works, including articles, book chapters, episodes on television or radio, poems, and short stories.

12. Italicize the titles of longer works, including album or CD titles, art pieces, books, films, journals, magazines, newspapers, and television shows.

13. Give the edition number for works with more than one edition [e.g., *Publication manual of the American Psychological Association* (6th ed.)].

14. Include the DOI (digital object identifier), a unique alpha-numeric string assigned by a registration agency that helps identify content and provides a link to the source online. All DOI numbers begin with a *10* and contain a prefix and suffix separated by a slash (for example, 10.11037/0278-6133.27.3.379). The DOI is usually found in the citation detail or on the first page of an electronic journal article near the copyright notice.

CITATION DETAIL WITH DOI

stet Detail

Title:

An Ability Traitor at Work: A Treasonous Call to Subvert *Writing* From Within.

Authors:

Holbrook, Teri[1] *tholbrook@gsu.edu*

Source:

Qualitative Inquiry; Mar2010, Vol. 16 Issue 3, p171-183, 13p

Document Type:

Article

Subject Terms:

*DISABILITIES

*QUALITATIVE research

*MANAGEMENT science

*SIGN language

*WRITING

Author-Supplied Keywords:

assemblage

disability

multigenre

multimodal writing

NAICS/Industry Codes:

541930 Translation and Interpretation Services

Abstract:

In questioning conventional qualitative research methods, St. Pierre asked, "What else might *writing* do except mean?" The author answers, it oppresses. Co-opting the race traitor figurative, she calls on qualitative researchers to become "ability traitors" who interrogate how a valuable coinage of their trade—the written word—is used to rank and categorize individuals with troubling effects. In this article, she commits three betrayals: (a) multigenre *writing* that undermines the authoritative text; (b) assemblage as a method of analysis that deprivileges the written word; and (c) a gesture toward a dis/comfort text intended to take up Lather's example of challenging the "usual ways of making sense." In committing these betrayals, the author articulates her "traitorous agenda" designed to interrogate assumptions about inquiry, power, equity, and *writing* as practice-as-usual. [ABSTRACT FROM AUTHOR]

Author Affiliations:
    [1]Georgia State University
ISSN:
    10778004
DOI:
    10.1177/1077800409351973
Accession Number:
    47934623
Database:
    Academic Search Premier
View Links:
    Find Fulltext

| 38f | **Formats for print sources** |

1. Books (includes brochures, pamphlets, and graphic novels)

Author's Last name, Author's Initial of first name. (Year of publication). *Title of book*. Place of publication: Publisher.

➜ Lansky, D. (2005). *Signspotting*. Oakland, CA: Lonely Planet.

> **Helpful hint**
>
> Only use the state after the city if the city is not a place that would be commonly known or if there may be more than one commonly known city by that name.

2. Books with two or more authors

A comma is used between the author names, even if there are only two authors.

First Author's Last name, First author's Initial of first name, & Second author's Last name, Second author's Initial of first name. (year of publication). *Title of book*. Place of publication: Publisher.

➜ Maasik, S., & Soloman, J. (2008). *Signs of life in the USA: Readings on popular culture for writers*. Boston, MA: Bedford/St. Martin's.

3. Two books by the same author

Be sure the entries are in sequential time order with earliest date first.

➜ Maasik, S., & Soloman, J. (2004). *California dreams and realities: Readings for critical thinkers and writers* (3rd ed.). Boston, MA: Bedford/St. Martin's.

➜ Maasik, S., & Soloman, J. (2008). *Signs of life in the USA: Readings on popular culture for writers*. Boston, MA: Bedford/St. Martin's.

4. Anthology or collection

Editor's Last name, Editor's Initial of first name. (Ed). (Year of publication). *Title of book.* Place of publication: Publisher.

→ Smith, A. D., Smith, T. G., & Wright, K. (Eds.). (2007). *COMPbiblio: Leaders and influences in composition theory and practice.* Southlake, TX: Fountainhead.

5. Work within an anthology or collection

Author's Last name, Author's Initial of first name. (Year of publication). Title of work. In Editor's Name(s) (Ed.) *Title of anthology* (page numbers). Place of publication: Publisher.

→ Tan, A. (2010). Mother tongue. In R. Bullock, M. D. Goggin, & F. Weinberg (Eds.). *The Norton field guide to writing* (pp. 564-70). New York, NY: Norton.

6. Article in a scholarly journal without DOI (digital object identifier)

Include the issue number if the journal is paginated by issue. If there is not a DOI available and the article was found online, give the URL of the journal home page.

Author's Last name, Author's Initial of first name. (Year of publication). Title of the article. *Journal Title, volume number* (issue number), pages. URL (if retrieved online).

→ Holbrook, T. (2010). An ability traitor at work: A treasonous call to subvert writing from within. *Qualitative Inquiry,* 16 (3), 171-183. Retrieved from E-Journals database.

7. Article in a scholarly journal with DOI (digital object identifier)

Author's Last name, Author's Initial of first name. (Year of publication). Title of the article. *Journal Title, volume number* (issue number), pages. doi:

→ Franks, L. (2006). The play in language. *Child Signs,* 73(1), 3-17. doi:10.1770/69873629

8. Article in a newspaper

Use *p.* or *pp.* before the page numbers in references of newspapers.

Note: if the newspaper article appears on discontinuous pages, be sure to give all the page numbers, separating them with a comma (e.g., pp. A4, A10, A13-14).

Author's Last name, Author's Initial of first name. (Year of publication, Month and Date of publication). Title of article. *Newspaper Title*, pp. page numbers.

➔ Genzlinger, N. (2010, April 6). Autism is another thing that families share. *The New York Times*, p. A4.

9. Article in a magazine

Author's Last name, Author's Initial of first name. (Year of publication, Month of publication). Title of article. *Magazine Title, volume number* (issue number), pages.

Note: only use day if magazine is published on a weekly or bi-weekly basis.

➔ Musico, C. (2009, November). Sign 'em up! *CRM Magazine, 13*(11), 49.

10. Review

Be sure to identify the type of work being reviewed by noting if it is a book, film, television program, painting, song, or other creative work. If the work is a book, include the author name(s) after the book title, separated by a comma. If the work is a film, song, or other media, be sure to include the year of release after the title of the work, separated by a comma.

Reviewer's Last name, Reviewer's Initial of first name. (Year of publication, Month and Date of Publication). Title of review [Review of the work *Title of work*, by Author's Name]. *Magazine or Journal Title, volume number* (issue number), pp. page numbers. doi number (if available).

➔ Turken, R. (2008, May 5). Life outside of the box. [Review of the film *Signs*, 2002]. *Leisure Times*, pp. A12.

11. Article in a reference book

Author's Last name, Author's Initial of first name. (Year of publication). Title of chapter or entry. In A. Editor (Ed). *Title of book* (pp. xx-xx). Location: Publisher.

➔ Jones, A. (2003). Semiotics. In B. Smith, R. Lore, and T. Rex (Eds.). *Encyclopedia of signs* (pp. 199-202). Boston, MA: Rutledge.

12. Religious and classical works

In APA, classical religious works, such as the Bible and the Qur'an, and major classical works that originated in Latin or Greek, are not required to have entries in the References list but should include reference to the text within the sentence in the essay. Note: it is always a good idea to check with your instructor on this type of entry since there can be some variety across instructors and schools.

38g Formats for online sources

1. Web site

The documentation form for a Web site can also be used for online message, blog, or video posts.

Author's Last name, Author's Initial of first name (if author given). (Year, Month Day). *Title of page* [Description of form]. Retrieved from http://www.xxxx

➔ United States Post Office (2010). *United States Post Office Services Locator* [search engine]. Retrieved from http://usps.whitepages.com/post_office

2. Article from a Web site, online newspaper, blog, or wiki (with author given)

Author's Last name, Author's Initial of first name. (Year, Month Day of publication). Title of article. *Name of Webpage/Journal/Newspaper*. Retrieved from http://www.xxxxxxx

→ Ebert, R. (2002, August 2). Signs. *Chicago Sun-Times*. Retrieved from http://rogerebert.suntimes.com/

3. Article from a Web site, online newspaper, blog, or wiki (with no author given)

Title of article. (Year, Month Day of publication). *Name of Webpage/Journal/Newspaper*. Retrieved from http://www.xxxxxxx

→ China's traditional dress: Qipao. (2001, October). *China Today*. Retrieved from http://chinatoday.com

4. Online journal article

The reference for an online journal article is set up the same way as for a print one, including the DOI.

Author's Last name, Author's Initial of first name. (Year of publication). Title of the article. *Journal Title, volume number* (issue number), pages. doi:xxxxxxxxxxxx

→ Franks, L. (2006). The play in language. *Child Signs*, 73(1), 3-17. doi:10.1770/69873629

If a DOI is not assigned to content you have retrieved online, use the home page URL for the journal or magazine in the reference (e.g., Retrieved from http://www.xxxxxx).

→ Austen, V. (2003). Writing spaces: Performance of the word. *Kairos*. Retrieved from http://kairos.com

5. Article from an online service, such as General One-File, LexisNexis, JSTOR, ERIC

When using APA, it is not necessary to include database information as long as you can include the publishing information required in a normal citation. Note: this is quite different from using MLA documentation, which requires full information about the database.

6. Article in an online reference work

Author's Last name, Author's Initial of first name. (Year of publication). Title of chapter or entry. In A. Editor (Ed). *Title of book.* Retrieved from http://xxxxxxxxxx

→Jones, A. (2003). Semiotics. In B. Smith, R. Lore, and T. Rex (Eds.). *Encyclopedia of signs.* Retrieved from http://brown.edu/signs

38h Formats for other commonly used sources

1. Television or radio program (single episode)

Writer' Last name, Writer's Initial of first name. (Writer), & Director's Last name, Director's Initial of first name. (Director). (Year). Title of episode [Television/Radio series episode]. In Executive Producer's name (Executive Producer), *Title of show.* Place: Network.

→Bell, J. (Writer), Carter, C. (Creator), & Manners, K. (Director). (2000). Signs and wonders [Television series episode]. In C. Carter (Executive Producer), *The X files.* New York, NY: FOX.

2. Sound recording

Writer's Last name, Writer's Initial of first name. (Copyright year). Title of song. [Recorded by Artist's name if different from writer]. On *Title of album* [Medium of recording]. Location: Label. (Date of recording if different from song copyright date).

→Emmerson, L. (1970). Signs. [Recorded by Five Man Electrical Band]. On *Good-byes and butterflies* [LP]. New York, NY: Lionel Records.

→Emmerson, L. (1970). Signs. [Recorded by Tesla]. On *Five man acoustical jam* [CD]. New York, NY: Geffen. 1990.

3. Film

Producer's Last name, Producer's Initial of first name. (Producer), & Director's Last name, Director's Initial of first name. (Director). (Year). *Title of film* [Motion picture]. Country of Origin: Studio.

➜ Kennedy, K. (Producer), & Shyamalan, M. N. (Director). (2002). *Signs* [film]. USA: Touchstone.

4. Painting, sculpture, or photograph

Artist's Last name, Artist's Initial of first name. (Year, Month Day). *Title of material*. [Description of material]. Name of collection (if available). Name of Repository, Location.

➜ Gainsborough, T. (1745). *Conversation in a park*. [Oil painting on canvas]. Louvre, Paris, France.

5. Personal interview

Unlike MLA documentation, personal interviews and other types of personal communication are not included in APA References lists. Be sure to cite personal communications in the text only.

6. Lecture, speech, address, or reading

Speaker's Last name, Speaker's Initial of first name. (Year, Month). Title of speech. *Event name*. Lecture conducted from Sponsor, Location.

➜ Stephens, L. (2009, December). The signs of the times. *MLA annual convention*. Lecture conducted from Hilton Hotel Downtown, New York, NY.

38i Sample References list using APA

Following is an example of how a completed References list would look at the end of your paper.

Your Last name   14

References

Emmerson, L. (1970). Signs. [Recorded by Five Man Electrical

Band]. On *Good-byes and butterflies* [LP]. New York,

NY: Lionel Records.

Franks, L. (2006). The play in language. *Child Signs*, 73(1), 3-17.

doi:10.1770/69873629

Kennedy, K. (Producer), & Shyamalan, M. N. (Director). (2002).

Signs [film]. USA: Touchstone.

Jones, A. (2003). Semiotics. In B. Smith, R. Lore, and T. Rex

(Eds.). *Encyclopedia of signs*. Retrieved from

http://brown.edu/signs

Lansky, D. (2005). *Signspotting*. Oakland, CA: Lonely Planet.

Stephens, L. (2009, December). The signs of the times. *MLA*

annual convention. Lecture conducted from Hilton Hotel

Downtown, New York, NY.

Tan, A. (2010). Mother tongue. In R. Bullock, M. D. Goggin, &

F. Weinberg (Eds.). *The Norton field guide to writing* (pp.

564-70). New York, NY: Norton.

New Media Literacy

How do digital practices—mostly, the things that we do when we interact with the Internet—affect our lives? We can look to our economic activity and observe how frequently people shop, pay their bills, and manage investments online. We choose restaurants, concerts, and films based on feedback that we receive digitally from both advertisers who don't know us and friends who do. Most of the work that you did to apply to this university probably happened online. Our culture is no longer fascinated by the existence of the Internet; in fact, we often take it for granted. However, the last five years of collaborative, social activity on the Internet is a subject of intense academic study right now. As the Internet shifted from a location where one could *receive* information to a place where one could *participate* in information, a new model of activity developed. This transformation is commonly called Web 2.0, a term that describes how online users have moved from consumption to production of content. This chapter will address how that consumption and production relates to the act of composing in your ENGL 1101 and 1102 courses at Georgia State University.

We should define an important term. "New media," we can loosely assert, are the host of programs, apps, and collectives that enable and produce participatory digital culture. Television and radio do not count as new media, but as soon as we say that, we see the boundaries of these concepts dissolving. Maybe you watch a program on NBC (a TV broadcasting network that started as RCA in 1926), but you watch over an ATT connection that is also your pipeline to the Internet. You might watch it on a television that, with one click, can enable browsing on the Web. More to the point, you might watch that NBC content on Hulu, the website that streams NBC's television content on the Web. Movies are technically not "new media," but they are certainly embedded in the culture of the Internet, considering the millions of people who stream movies from Netflix or watch movie trailers on YouTube every day. New media certainly interacts with and cross-pollinates with "old media" (as silly as that sounds), but the defining quality of new media forms is engagement. Pre-Internet media produced static content; new media invite and depend on *user content*.

"Usage Error" by Michael Black-Akert

For Thought and Discussion

Consider how the Internet delivers new media to users who may or may not have the digital experience to interpret those media.

This section will address how three terms in digital culture have an impact on our work as critical thinkers and composers. We will examine *attention*, *participation*, and *audience* in the context of new media and the composition classroom.

ATTENTION

Early computer users sat down to their boxy towers with specific tasks in mind—"I will write an email," for instance. Increasingly, the phrase "sitting down at a computer" seems antiquated, as many of us carry the functionality of a small computer around in our pockets. Our cellphones can quickly gain and delete new programs (apps), connect us to instantaneous live conversation (Twitter or chat programs), and sometimes serve as one of our main sources of media consumption. Whether you consider your cellphone or tablet, your laptop or the desktop computer in the library's digital commons, you are rarely removed from the constant stream of multimedia content that the Internet provides. How does this stream, sometimes a flood, affect our academic work, our theory of knowledge, or our control over our activities? In short, how does being five seconds away from the Web impact our attention?

You might not find it surprising that interest in the field of neuroscience has increased parallel to our digital activity. After all, the more we learn about the world through our computers, the more we have to think about how we manage that learning and how it impacts our future learning. For example, you may think that the Internet automatically provides you with a wider lens on world events than citizens had before the Internet. Back then, radio, television, and newspaper media held control over what most people could realistically "know" outside of their own experience. With the Internet—blogs, Twitter, online newspapers, YouTube, etc.—you might be tempted to say that that control has been transformed. Now, you can learn anything that you want. However, consider what happens when we decide to follow someone on Twitter or friend them on Facebook, when we add a blog to our RSS reader account or subscribe to a YouTube channel. We are selecting or curating our own list of regularly updated media. However, if we collect that list according to our pre-existing and unexamined tastes, we are essentially avoiding Web content that we feel is irrelevant. Our curation, if not reflective, can put a boundary around our learning.

Therefore, attention involves what media we attend to. It also involves *how* we pay attention. A variety of studies over the last several years have attempted to understand whether we learn differently when we use digital technologies. Consider the iPad or the Kindle, even the laptop; are these items ideal for reading specific kinds of material and not for others? Given that many of us work these days with several Internet browser windows up at the same time, we toggle back and forth among several sites: email, social media (like Facebook or Twitter), research, and writing. We chat with our collaborative partner who posts a link to a *New York Times* story, which links to an academic study, which in turn includes a graph that we want to drop into our presentation. That process entails several steps, but we move through them without much effort and without thinking about the implications of all of those windows, all of those platforms.

In *Net Smart: How To Thrive Online*, Howard Rheingold describes what he calls "infotention": "intention added to attention, and mixed with knowledge of information-filtering … a coordinated mind-machine process" (17). Rheingold explores how digital, networked activity strains our attention in unique ways, and we should train our brain to be more focused when we

"The Associates" by Judith Kim

do work online. Cathy Davidson suggests, on her syllabus for "This Is Your Brain on The Internet," an interdisciplinary undergraduate course at Duke University, that if the metaphor for the brain in the 20th century was the CPU, then the brain metaphor for the 21st century is the iPhone. Think about it. The iPhone works across multiple platforms and applications, it organizes networks, and it shares data in a variety of different forms. Its strength as a piece of technology is its ability to connect pathways among a variety of different programs and applications.

One of Rheingold's goals in *Net Smart* is to get people thinking about how to exercise control and focus over their attention during online work. Many of us have had the experience of sitting down "just for a minute" to Facebook, YouTube, or Tumblr and discovering two hours and multiple browser windows later that we have no idea where the time went. Consider our compulsive reaching for cellphones and our instinctive clicking on hyperlinks in a news story, just to satisfy curiosity or, deeper, to fulfill a less explicable psychological "need." In *Alone Together: How We Expect More from Technology and Less from Each Other*, Sherry Turkle studies the psychological complexity of human/computer relationships. She worries about the effect of "always on/always on you" networked devices on our ability to attend to others, to listen, and to empathize.

Is paying attention or staying focused while online difficult for you? Take a minute to examine your ability to monitor your attention online by trying some of the exercises below.

- Find a friend who will let you study an "hour" of his or her online time. Take notes on where your friend goes, how many browser windows are kept open, and where links lead. Collect the raw "data" on what your friend consumes and produces (status updates, tweets, and emails count as "production"). After you are finished, try organizing the data: Into what categories can you divide the visited sites? Where did your subject spend the most time? Did activity seem linear (progressing along a logical path) or more organic or impulsive? Ask your subject to record the same "data" for you and discuss what you find. What does it teach you?

- Research the Pomodoro Technique of time management and the application Focus Booster (www.focusbosterapp.com). Divide your time online into 25-minute segments according to Pomodoro and write realistic goals for what you are going to do during the time period (whether or not for academic purposes). How successful were you at staying on task for three different time segments?

- Read John Tierney's article "When the Mind Wanders, Happiness Also Strays" in *The New York Times* (Nov 15, 2010) and Jocelyn K. Glie's post "10 Online Tools for Better Attention and Focus" on the productivity website *99%*. Experiment with some of the tools and compose a response to both texts that is personal to your own experiences online. Do Glie's and Tierney's pieces convince you that time spent wandering online is a problem to solve?

For Thought and Discussion

> Our attention is demanded in our physical and virtual lives. How does a trip across the GSU quad focus our attention in ways that online activity does not?

The iPhone connects different media just like the brain makes connections among different languages, senses, social groups and activities. However, our brain works differently from a machine in that it can pay attention to only one process at a time when we ask it to complete something complicated. Before we begin an investigation of reading new kinds of media, it behooves us to acknowledge the challenges of that exploration. Do digital consumption and production encourage us, as Nicholas Carr writes in *The Shallows: What the Internet Is Doing To Our Brains*, "to dip in and out of a series of texts rather than devote sustained attention to any one of them," or is the abundance of information beneficial, according to Clay Shirky's *Here Comes Everybody*? Either way, as citizens of the virtual world, investigating the question becomes imperative. Rheingold writes that "[j]ust as the ancient arts of rhetoric taught citizens how to construct and weigh arguments, a mindful rhetoric of digital search would concentrate attention on the process of inquiry—the kinds of questions people turn into initial search queries" (64).

PARTICIPATION

Our early uses of the Web involved an excited amount of access to information—information that was always available and timely. Schools, businesses, non-profit organizations, the government, any organized group could publish current data about its work. The Internet was supremely useful for checking movie times, ordering gifts, and generally just "finding things."

As time progressed, however, the Web became more dynamic. The O'Reilly Media Web 2.0 Conference, started in 2004, introduced the term "Web 2.0" into common usage. "Web 2.0" distinguishes between prior uses of the Web that were mainly consumptive and the evolving ability of digital citizens to *produce content*.

Plenty of people participated in digital culture before 2005, but after that time the Internet became more participation-friendly. Facebook, Wikipedia, and Flickr, among many others, signaled a new orientation for digital culture: they encourage user-generated content. Just think—what is Facebook without the pictures and text that its users contribute? Not much. It simply provides a very attractive and share-able frame that users are happy to populate with their own content. The shift in digital culture designated "Web 2.0" is significant, even if no one really agrees when it officially started (or if it has already ceded to some new model). Think of the stereotypical couch potato watching television for hours; this person illustrates the once passive media consumer. While being online may not appear any more physically active, online activity is now a thoroughly more interactive way to engage with media.

We can think of all this "production" actually as a new form of publishing; comments on an *Atlanta Journal and Constitution* editorial, posts to a blog, reviews of a book on Amazon, pictures to Picasa, or posting videos to YouTube represent dissemination of your thoughts. If everyone is publishing more, then everyone must be composing more; the inherent goals of first-year composition begin here. You may not think that a "writing" class has any relationship to how you interact with the Web, but think for a minute: is there another environment, apart from the web, where you write more?

Consider Wikipedia. Perhaps the most useful participatory experiment on the Web, Wikipedia presents an open model for knowledge production. We can all contribute to its vastness. In the early days of Wikipedia, teachers often scolded students for using Wikipedia in any scholarly way (many still do, in fact). However, Wikipedia has developed from a collection of thousands of dubious, argumentative posts to millions of entries that are constantly under revision by the citizens of the Web. Wikipedia is still not a recommended source in an academic essay, but it can be a great starting point when you begin to write something new. Wikipedia entries provide links to other, more verifiable sources, and these sources provide researchers additional places to search for credible content. If managed carefully and critically, mass-crowd participation can produce infinitely useful media on the Web. The lesson we learn from Wikipedia is this: our participation, as minor as it may seem, remains important to the digital environment because other people can quickly access it, comment upon it, remix it, or engage us in conversation about it.

For Thought and Discussion

Wikipedia, in its ability to open construction of "stable" knowledge to a variety of digital users, suggests a new culture of comment, revision, and re-imagination. What other websites offer new cultures to their users? Describe the "cultures" of these websites.

Because participation has become an integral component of Web culture, it behooves us to understand and assimilate it with our own behavior, if and when appropriate. This strategy means moving from a place of consumption (reading a restaurant review) to production (writing a review ourselves after our visit). The Internet has become such a useful collection of media *because* millions of people have taken it upon themselves to contribute to it. These discrete and numerous contributions to the content of the Internet result in enormous cultural changes to publishing, journalism, entertainment, and education. On a deeper level, they have an influence on how our culture defines "knowledge."

When we interact with the content of the Web, we encourage more interactivity and connection. When we post pictures or comments to our friends' content on Facebook, others can reply and we can start a conversation.

"0100101001001" by Fenton Thompson

We learn from social media, on an unconscious level, that the more we put into it, the more we get out of it. The content of our contributions to social media networks, and to the Web in general, has a large impact on response. If we type "great pics!" to a new album that someone has uploaded to Google+, we will probably not get much response. However, if we engage the photos in some creative or narrative way, other people on the network are more prone to participate with us. We might post "this picture reminds me of that time that we all met for dinner at Eats; when was that? who was there?" and with that, the digital "ball" starts rolling. Other people within the network are encouraged to answer the questions, link to more pictures, or make their own reflections.

The important lesson for the composition class, and any academic experience for that matter, is that participation increases our engagement in learning and connects us to other people. Discussion boards are a common feature of digital education portals (like Blackboard, Web CT, Desire

2 Learn, etc.), and teachers who use them are encouraging engagement and community. Rather than contributing an answer that is flat, we should approach a forum like we do a conversation—validating the opinions of others, making distinctions, and encouraging more response. Consider the following exchange in a hypothetical class:

Prompt: "How are the lessons of this lab useful?"

> *Melora: I found this lab useful because it helped me answer questions that will be on the test.*

> *Jack: The lab was difficult because I kept getting different results from the tests. Was I doing it wrong?*

Do you have experience in the participatory culture of the Web or does it seem foreign to you? Here are some suggestions of how you can explore the dynamic capabilities of the Web.

- Choose a recent online article in *The Atlanta Journal and Constitution* (www.ajc.com) or *Creative Loafing* (www.clatl.com) that includes a number of comments. Read through the comment chain, and post a response that agrees or disagrees with the contributions of previous commenters, citing their user names. See if you can get a discussion going between you and the community around the article to further explore the topic. Remember: engage in dissent civilly and carefully. Your goal is to encourage courteous, intelligent discussion.

- Use an online discussion forum provided by your instructor to identify classmates who share your interest in a genre of music, film, or literature. Use the open-endedness of the prompt to practice community engagement: ask others to clarify statements that interest you and try to make overt connections between your interests and theirs. Analyze the thread in order to determine who makes the most engaging comments that move others toward participation.

- Conduct a scavenger hunt related to material for your class via one social media network. Post the list of the items across the platform in a way that allows team members to share information (pictures of items acquired, interesting interactions, etc.) dynamically. Analyze which team's platform or use of the platform best supported the experience.

Ahmad: I had the same experience as Jack, but I think that is part of the conclusion actually. If the results of the various tests are not consistent, doesn't that mean that we should consider outside variables?

Stephanie: I agree with Ahmad: like time of day, how the testing might change after multiple uses, temperature?

In this exchange, Melora interacts like a passive consumer. She gives the instructor back the answer that she thinks he is seeking. Jack, Ahmad, and Stephanie however, approach the forum with questions, suggestions, and connections. They express an intuitive value in the scholarly members of the forum community, and they participate in ways that foreground critical thinking, citation, and community. Our active and critical participation in digital environments, whether on the open Web or on classroom projects, are valuable to others. Digital culture invests knowledge sharing and knowledge production with more democratic potential, and we should take these opportunities seriously. On the next class discussion forum, peer review assignment, or information gathering trip across the Web, consider how your participation helps others. If you have something to contribute, think critically about how to provide comments in a detailed way that encourages community and interaction.

AUDIENCE

Audience has always been one of the trickiest issues for a writer to consider. Once, the audience for any text was limited to those who had economic access to the work, geographic proximity, and interest in the text. Whether it was the newspaper or a physics textbook, all three of those variables had to line up for us to begin to think about audience. Does someone have the money to buy the text or the ability to borrow it? Can someone physically get to where the text is located? Who is interested in this text? These questions acted as controlling factors, limiting and shaping an audience.

For Thought or Discussion

An artist often has to work hard to "find" her audience, even to the point of relocation. How does the Internet affect how a composition can find an audience?

The digital landscape has blurred or erased all of those variables. Certainly people still purchase texts, but the fact that texts *can* be obtained

"Blue Maniac" by Courtney Jane Richir

for free has resulted in millions of people writing content without asking for payment (consider the blogosphere, for example). The limits of physical geography are rendered almost irrelevant for readers with an Internet connection. Whether you buy a book on your Kindle or access articles on *The New Yorker* for free, that content is digitally available in seconds. Finally, there's the question of interest. Audiences are still limited to those who have an interest in the text, but because of the lowered thresholds of the first two (economic and geographic access) digital citizens can afford to be interested in more topics. The concept of digital searches (Google as the most ubiquitous, but not the only, example) has increased the amount of content to which an Internet user is exposed; consequently, we see that traditional limitations on a text's audience are dissolving.

But composers still have to consider audience, just as traditional writers have done. They just have to consider other factors as well. If the barrier to obtaining texts is dissolving and readers have more access to them, the new barrier that takes its place is *attention*. Every person who regularly spends time online knows that there are exponentially more free texts readily available and interesting enough to read than she will ever be able to read. So a reader's free time becomes a limiting factor. So, also does interactivity. Most users prefer to read texts with which they can interact— comment on, share, amend.

Composers in digital spaces should comprehend these new limits, motivations, and definitions of audience. Traditionally, anyone desiring to publish in a specific community needs to study the conventions, style, and content of that community. In the new media environment, that responsibility extends to forms of media. Specific composing platforms attract and engage unique audiences and construct unique community protocols. We are going to look at two of these in order to explore how they require a new definition of audience.

Blogs

The simplest tool for mass communication online is a weblog, commonly known as a *blog*. Multiple platforms (Wordpress, Blogger, LiveScribe, and many others) offer users a free space to construct multimedia compositions and publish them to the Web. Because blogging is so accessible and so many blogs exist, each successful blog speaks to a specific community and endeavors to cultivate that sense of community. Certainly, some blogs cater to a large, diverse audience—like blogs associated with CNN or the *New York Times*—but even those are tailored to specific readers within that network (example: the CNN religion blog).

Authors in the blogosphere spend time studying blogs addressed to similar audiences. In fact, most blogs feature a "blog roll" of other authors with whom they share affinity. This familiarity with similar digital spaces may not seem very much like academic "research," but it works the same way. Unless an author is lucky, he usually needs to discover and cultivate relationships with the authors within his interest network.

As all successful digital texts have become participatory, a blog is only partly the rhetorical territory of the author. The commenting space of successful blogs is alive with the responses of regular readers who voice support, critique, or extensions of the author's work. Different from a more traditional medium—the book—the authorial content of the blog is often influenced by the participation of its readers. Bloggers across a number of topics—academic, professional, or social—compose blog entries in response to the communities that develops around their sites. Active commenters on the blog form a dynamic audience that most bloggers appreciate and, to a great or minor degree, study.

Twitter

First launched in 2006, Twitter is the most popular microblogging platform online and is currently the second most popular social media site on the

Internet. Like most social media sites, Twitter forces composers to consider audience in new and dynamic ways. Twitter users construct their own audience through an open network of other users and "hashtag" searches. More importantly, as is the case with most social media networks, Twitter users are both authors and audience members. As they post tweets, they cultivate the attention of other users. Twitter's unique place in the social media sphere is defined by its mostly open network and the compressed size of each tweet.

Twitter has evolved into a mostly public network, different from other platforms where users choose others who can see their content. While Twitter users have the option to "lock" their tweets, the platform encourages sharing information openly with the Web at large. Most Twitter users compose tweets with the understanding that they might be read by anyone, potentially lots of people they don't know. Twitter's "retweet" function permits a user to send a tweet to all of his followers with one click; if any of those readers also retweet that content, one author's contribution to the open network can quickly become viral.

The size of tweets also contributes significantly to an understanding of audience. A post to the Twitter network is limited to 140 characters, a limit which demands brevity. As we discussed before, the free access to information on the Web means that users are limited by the amount of media they can realistically digest. Blog posts and news articles can take minutes to digest, whereas a Twitter user can realistically read dozens of tweets during a five-minute period. This kind of reading is not thorough, but it does not need to be. Twitter users quickly develop an understanding of the usefulness of the network and can discard large amounts of what they read in order to get to information that is personally or professionally valuable. Because tweets can include links to more developed content, Twitter can become a suggestion board for longer texts.

For Thought or Discussion

Twitter messages can reach a ready audience in seconds with updated information about a local gathering, news worthy event, or protest. Police have used Twitter in order to keep informed of mounting protests or safety issues. What are some other professions that use social media like Twitter extensively? Why is audience an important consideration when using social media, especially in the professional realm?

The new media available to digital composers require a revised understanding of audience. When we compose for online spaces, whether a

"Update" by Judith Kim

long-form blog post or a short tweet, we should do so with an appreciation for their potential interactivity and reach. Active digital readers want to participate in the texts that interest them, and the best Web compositions court that kind of participation. If you are assigned to compose a digital text for your class, pose questions that invite the replies of your readers. Open questions will suffice, but your post should steer readers toward a particular understanding and ask pointed questions about it. For example, your professor may ask you to respond to a reading from the textbook in a discussion forum open to the class; compose a text that explores the trickier questions of the reading. Do not be afraid to "think out loud" about what seems contradictory in the reading or about what terminology is unclear. Discussion forums, blog posts, and tweets are never intended to be closed circuit communication. They engage in constructing knowledge through participation and engagement.

While the use of new media in your composition classroom may be new to you, many professors are beginning to use new media sites or practices. College students have always had to embrace their identities as writers to be successful. New media spheres encourage us to think of ourselves as composers, too: of conversations, of visual images, of research projects. Digital learning, whether in a physical class that uses an online portal or a hybrid or fully online course, asks us to employ skills that we have already learned and to evaluate them critically. Exploring the definitions of atten-

Consider how these exercises prompt you to rethink the idea of "audience" across the Web.

- Choose a regular blogger in a topic you enjoy (fashion, film, religion, politics, travel) who also maintains a Twitter presence. Spend some time researching who follows the author's Twitter account and who follows the blog. Are they the same people or are there some clear differences? Is one group significantly larger than another? What contrast exists between the topics of the blog posts and the content of the blogger's tweets? Often you will find that bloggers use Twitter to inform readers of new posts, but often the tweets will wander into different topics. Contrast the author's interaction with audience members between the blog and Twitter account.

- Read Clive Thompson's *Wired* article "How Twitter Creates a Social Sixth Sense," published only a year after Twitter's launch. Then read Katrina Gulliver's "10 Commandments of Twitter for Academics," published in 2012 in *The Chronicle of Higher Education*. Thompson's article displays no comments (this feature has been closed by *Wired*), but Gulliver's article includes long responses. How do each of these authors attend to the idea of audience within the Twitter platform?

- Choose a YouTube video that you find hilarious—you know, one of those memes that everyone sees within a 2-week period—and a blog post from any regularly posting author. How do the comments attached to one relate to the comments attached to the other? Analyze the difference between the two groups. While the video may have thousands of comments, evaluate the amount of engagement each audience has with the content. How does the composer's relationship with the audience affect its engagement?

tion, participation, and audience within a new media context helps us make sense of an increasingly digital world. Gaining new media fluency is an essential part of our development as critical thinkers, writers, and composers.

FOR FURTHER READING

For more on digital media and on the production of digital texts in the Web 2.0 environment, take a look at these sources:

The Agenda with Steve Paikin: *The Myth of Digital Literacy* (video)

John Brockman: *Is the Internet Changing the Way You Think?* (book)

Collin Brooke: *Lingua Fracta* (book)

Nicholas Carr: *The Shallows: What the Internet Is Doing To Our Brains* (book)

Tyler Cowan: "Three Tweets for the Web" (article)

Cathy Davidson: *Now You See It* (book)

David Eagleman: *Six Easy Steps to Avert the Collapse of Civilization* (video lecture)

Howard Rheingold: *Net Smart: How To Thrive Online* (book)

Clay Shirky: *Here Comes Everybody* (book)

Sherry Turkle: *Alone Together* (book)

STUDENT WORK

To find out more about producing digital texts, please visit **www.guidetowriting.gsu.edu**. Click on "Community," then "Resource Sharing," then "Digital Projects." Here, you will find student examples of digital composition. Produce your own digital creations and share the links with the webmaster. She will add your work to our website to expand your audience.

Writing through Culture

In the first-year writing program, instructors may recommend researching and writing about culture as a means for exploring different genres of writing. Cultural writing also invites experimentation with language as we adapt to the needs of an audience of academic peers.

The *Oxford English Dictionary* defines **culture** as "the distinctive ideas, customs, social behavior, products, or way of life of a particular nation, society, people, or period." The ideas that organize culture can serve as promising topics in the first-year writing program because the connections between writing and culture are changeable and can influence both individuals and groups. In other words, writing about culture can result in a measurable impact on local, national, and even global arenas.

If given the option to develop their own topics for writing and research in English 1101 and 1102, students may choose to write about culture for the unique opportunities it presents. For example, writers can explore their relationship with surrounding communities, and writing about culture empowers students to write with authority based on personal experiences and observations. Furthermore, engaging culture provides writers the opportunity to realize **praxis**, that is, writing or speaking to affect change. **Praxis** goes beyond what is often termed "best practices" to include an emphasis on rhetorical elements of a communicative situation. It is the practice of writing in the right place at the right moment to produce the most optimal outcome. In this mode, cultural writers write with a purpose, often either to change or preserve what they see. Ideally, writing about culture can lead to the realization that topics of scholarship are all around us, among the everyday people, places, and artifacts we encounter.

Entering a discussion about culture can be disorienting at first. Where does culture exist? How do we find our way in? While some cultural markers are obvious—protests and demonstrations, political debates and legislation, religious and spiritual gatherings, or even the flicker of news broadcasts from cable networks—culture also moves through our streets in smaller ways. For example, consider the places and spaces you access while attending college in the urban core of Atlanta. Just standing in the middle of Woodruff Park you are likely to see locals playing oversize chess, artists displaying their work, musicians improvising new riffs, construction workers improving the streets, and a steady stream of students, business professionals, and urban nomads all intermingling. Each of these scenes observed from Woodruff Park reveals a small glimpse into a rich cultural story.

Everyday culture in everyday places can be excavated to produce academic writing. This type of writing intersects with **cultural studies** in that it investigates the beliefs, values, and traditions of a society in order to better understand the lived experience of members within that society. To access that lived experience, a cultural writer has three main entry points: the **people** who are part of the culture, the **place** where the culture resides, and the **artifacts** made by members within the culture.

"GSU's Dragon" by Courtney Anderson

ENTRY POINT: CULTURE AND PEOPLE

When writers investigate **culture**, they grapple with questions about their personal experiences and those of other people within a particular community. Responding to these questions inevitably encourages us to reflect upon our own position within our community and even the world at large. These questions may relate to our feelings about a particular community: for example, does participation in the community's events feel freeing or restrictive, inspiring or discouraging? Or, they may lead us to examine the roles we inhabit within this particular community: are we leaders or followers, mediators or rebels? Most importantly, these questions may explore or reveal the dynamics of our relationships with other people within the community. This section discusses our responsibility to establish and maintain our relationships with people within the cultures we are studying.

Culture cannot exist without people. Ultimately, we are the agents of creation, transmission, and change in our culture. As we begin to write about culture, a logical starting point is to locate our own position within culture, often referred to as establishing our **_positionality_**. We construct our relationship to the topic at hand by considering our personal demographic information: gender, age, nationality, race, and ethnicity. To this information we add notes about our background: where we grew up, our education, religious/spiritual affiliations, and relevant economic factors. As we review this material, we may come to find it connects us in sometimes surprising ways to multiple communities. In other words, we might find a high school education in a suburb of Atlanta connects us to one community, while our membership at a local synagogue includes us in a different community. Sometimes these communities overlap, and sometimes we find ourselves participating in ever-widening networks of communities. A study of positionality can also reveal our proximity to communities of which we are not members. Consciously adopting a position either as an insider or outsider can be productive for cultural research and writing. These positions are typically referred to as _emic_ (insider) and _etic_ (outsider).

Doing the Right Thing: Ethics and Cultural Writing

When writing about culture, it is important to remember that you are working with the beliefs, values, and traditions that shape a group's entire way of life. Writing about something as sacred as others' beliefs can be fraught with ethical dilemmas: Have I represented these beliefs accurately? Have I portrayed them in a way that demonstrates respect for those who hold these beliefs? Has my writing done only good, and not harm, to the members of the culture? Remember that *a cultural writer is NOT an investigative reporter*. Your goal is never to *expose* but rather to *understand* and to help your readers do the same.

For this reason, **we strongly recommend that you select a culture to which you already belong**. Doing so ensures that you already have a strong sense of the culture's fundamental beliefs before you research more nuanced issues.

In addition to selecting a culture to which you already belong, the following are a few general reminders about our responsibilities as cultural writers and researchers. Writers of culture:

- sustain an appreciation for values/traditions that are not their own
- work intentionally for the benefit of the people and places they study
- find opportunities to give back to the community
- resist exploitative "exposé" research methods
- avoid objectifying research subjects

ENTRY POINT: CULTURE AND PLACES

What do you see when you look at your surroundings? Your home, whether your GSU dorm room or a house shared with your nuclear family, is simultaneously the site of your everyday life and an expression of culture. Home is, after all, a place you have marked as your own (even if only for the next four years). As a physical location, it also marks a space in an urban, multicultural campus in a large metropolitan area. These are not empty, homogenous spaces; these are culturally-infused, dynamic strata we can read as texts that produce academic discourse.

As discussed in Chapter Five, online spaces are proliferating rapidly in our society, and our presence in those spaces consumes more and more of our attention, whether by preference or necessity. These online spaces offer entirely different opportunities for cultural study. We could enter, for example, the GSU English Major Facebook page (https://www.facebook.com/EnglishDepartmentGSU) to get a glimpse of the activities of our peers, or we might leave traces of our presence in the Department's Twitter feed (https://twitter.com/GSU_English). In either example, we might ask ourselves how our digital traces affect online spaces and how these digital traces will manifest in the physical spaces we inhabit.

"Stranger" by Lillia Tran

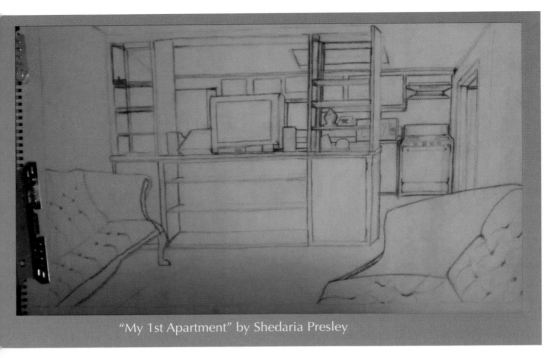

"My 1st Apartment" by Shedaria Presley

Exploring Culture and Place through Field Research and Writing

Connections between research and writing in a study of culture manifest in places familiar to many GSU students. Pause for a moment to reflect on your most recent visit to the Panthers Club food court located in the GSU University Center. Do you remember feeling satisfied with the choices available to you? Were the prices reasonable, the location hygienic, the offerings nutritious and appetizing? Comparing the menus at the various food stations presents you with the opportunity to first analyze primary sources and then draw inferences from their contents. These inferences carry signals about campus culture, and they are filtered through your unique perspective. It is important to remember that your eyes are interpreting what you see based on the particular culture in which you grew up, and inevitably, your interpretation is context specific, not universal. For example, observations about menu offering at Panthers Club cannot necessarily be applied to other GSU dining facilities, nor to dining facilities at other universities. Furthermore, if the cultural writer who observes Panthers Club's menus is vegan, her inferences will necessarily differ from those of a vegetarian writer. Because we are all inherently biased in some way, acknowledging your positionality and specifying the context of your observations supports responsible research and writing. Ultimately, the information you gather and the inferences you make can be shaped into writing that takes action. Your writing could develop into an evaluative essay in your first-year writing class or an informative blog post intended to advise other first-year students how to make the most of campus resources.

Writing inspired by observations and research on culture is purposeful and dynamic: it works to accomplish something, and it changes over time. Take for example the project described in the previous paragraph. What would happen if you approched that evaluative essay about the Panthers Club as a starting point, rather than an end point (merely an assignment that earns a grade)? Viewing your completed essay as a starting point for more critical thinking on culture could prompt you to conduct further research on the topic later in the semester, or even in other college courses. Seen this way, the essay becomes a platform on which to build knowledge, research, and additional writing. This strategy also makes sense from a practical standpoint (you don't have to "recreate the wheel" when you start on a new assign-ment). But how do you get started?

Here's an example of one of the many possible directions your work could take if you use the initial evaluative essay as a starting point. One option would be to expand your food investigation beyond the GSU campus into a wider cultural space such as the neighborhood at large. As practice, grab a notebook and pen and walk over to the Sweet Auburn Curb Market to exam-ine the food options in this neighborhood spot. Take the time to record what you see carefully in a set of *field notes* and create a *map* of the space where you will conduct your field research. You can then perform an analysis of

Tips for writing *field notes:*
1. Label your page with the date, time, location, and subject of your research.
2. Divide the page in half by drawing a line from top to bottom, creating two columns.
3. Label one column "Direct Observations." This column is the place for concrete, measurable, objective observations.
4. Label the other column "Personal Responses." This column is the place for your own thoughts, feelings, and any questions that arise during your note-taking session.
5. Field notes are most useful when you take the time to write *about* them. In other words, review both columns of notes, and then *write about what you see there.* Pay special attention to patterns, repetitions, and opportunities for further study.

your observations and draw some conclusions about the similarities and differences that you recognize.

During your visit to Sweet Auburn Curb Market, you might begin by asking what your observations lead you to believe about food in the area surrounding the GSU campus. What do the restaurants, food stands, and markets communicate about the culture of the neighborhood? Consider the languages and fragrances around you. As you look around, pay attention to small details like how the quinoa looks next to other grains and herbal medicine sticks. If you can, sample something that is new to you. How do these cultural markers compare to those you observed in the Panthers Club? The results of this comparison could lead to writing either of the following two documents: an op-ed piece for *The Signal* urging the GSU community to patronize the Market in order to keep our food culture vibrant, or a proposal to the SGA to lobby for new food stations in the dining halls that would more accurately represent GSU's multicultural population.

"Go" by James Supreme

Tips for *mapping* spaces in field research:

1. Select one of the places you visit on a daily basis (maybe GSU's library, shuttle system, or your place of employment). Be mindful about your choice of place and ask yourself the following questions: Does this place require special permission for entry? Is admission free and safe? Your selection process should begin with a quick set of notes on your assumptions about the location and the people who frequent it prior to starting your map.
2. Once you arrive at the site, spend some time observing spaces and people around you. Take notes on what you see, including descriptions of activity. Then draw a map or diagram of the space; be sure to mark the flow of movement and interactions of people within the space.
3. Write up your initial responses to your field notes and map immediately after leaving the location while your memory of it is fresh.

Place and Primary Sources

As introduced in Chapter Four, primary sources are frequently an integral part of the research process. Responding to cultural places gives you the opportunity both to study existing primary sources and create your own on topics relevant to your life. As we are about to see, identifying primary sources on cultural places can push you to think more broadly about what constitutes a "source," but this challenge is ultimately productive in that it allows for a good bit of freedom in approaching your research.

Another Atlanta place that could produce a rich cultural study of primary sources is the Krog Street Tunnel. Located just a few miles from GSU's campus, this tunnel has been the focus of much local attention, controversy, and conversation. Built in 1912, the tunnel provides a route beneath railroad tracks and forms the boundary between the affluent Inman Park neighborhood and a smaller, gentrifying mill village called Cabbagetown. (The origin of Cabbagetown's unique name continues to be the source of speculation, as it once housed the workers of Fulton Bag and Cotton Mills.) Atlanta's *Creative Loafing* boasts of the Krog Street Tunnel as "the original social networking site" for its collection of posters, messages, and graffiti art. (To read the article in its entirety, check out *Creative Loafing*'s website at clatl.com. You can follow the tunnel's daily transformations at http://the-dailykrog.tumblr.com/.) This cultural place lends itself to multiple research projects supported by primary sources in the form of art, text, architecture, newspaper coverage, exchanges over social media, even conversations on Cabbagetown's neighborhood email listserv.

"Krog Street Tunnel" by Jiri Vala Jr.

Regardless of the cultural site you select to study, you are not bound to engage solely with existing primary sources. The option always exists to generate your own primary sources, especially if you find existing sources do not open a course of investigation that interests you. For example, if you were intrigued by the Krog Street Tunnel but had the hunch that more could be learned from researching the Cabbagetown residents' real feelings about the graffiti on their neighborhood walls, that hunch might prove to be a productive point in your research process. From here, you have any number of options for creating primary sources that will reveal the information you seek. You might write a set of questions and interview members of the neighborhood association (often a place where community-minded individuals donate their time). You might also write a survey and distribute it throughout the neighborhood in order to get a broader perspective from a larger number of residents. No matter what you choose to do, using pre-existing primary sources or creating your own can lead to engaging, innovative research, allowing you to explore your interests while producing new knowledge about local cultural places.

Examples of ways to create primary sources:

1. Conduct interviews.
2. Write and distribute surveys.
3. Record your own observations and experiments.
4. Start a Twitter exchange based on a hashtag of your choice, or start a blog on a topic of your choice and invite others to contribute.
5. Build your own archive of images or artifacts.

ENTRY POINT: CULTURE AND ARTIFACTS

Using artifacts as an entry point to studying culture may seem at the outset to be an easier task than researching cultural places, but the challenges that these types of writing projects present simply test writers in different ways. Working with *artifacts* or material objects made by human beings (rather than those produced by nature) means employing evidence of *material culture*. These cultural "texts" can take the form of clothes, jewelry, furniture, sports equipment, tools, or any other object from everyday life, and they often bear a rich cultural history. When writing about artifacts, we frequently are prompted to scan these texts for deeper meanings (recall our discussion of text analysis in Chapter Two).

One way to uncover these deeper meanings is through *sensory description* in academic writing. First, keep in mind that instructors will often request "more details" or ask you to "make this paragraph more descriptive." Your instructor likely is asking you to engage one or more of your five senses. When you have a concrete object in front of you, this task becomes more manageable. Simply begin with one of your five senses and use it as a *lens* (or mode of seeing). For example, imagine you are holding in your hands the object depicted in "Celebrating Life" (see image on page 172). How would it feel to the touch? You would then list your findings (perhaps it would be lightweight, delicate, dry, rough around the edges) and then move on to one of the four remaining senses. Or you could return to your field notes on that trip to the Sweet Auburn Curb Market. Did the smell or appearance of an unfamiliar food lead you to purchase and try it? How did you describe the taste of the food? Collecting this type of data builds a bank of sensory details from which you can generate descriptive writing.

"Celebrating Life" by Lorelei Crystalilly Marden

Any discussion of material culture and cultural artifacts in contemporary society benefits from recognizing that we live in a world that increasingly focuses its attention on screens: screens attached to TVs, movies, computers, or phones. Screen time" absorbs more and more of our time, and because visual media is a product of culture, it can also serve as a productive cultural artifact for analysis. Below is an example of how one student writer at GSU approached an instructor's prompt using a television show as a cultural artifact.

SAMPLE ASSIGNMENT

The following is an example of a typical first-year writing prompt from instructor Jessica Temple's English 1102 course. Her student Jessica Martinez successfully composed a response to this writing prompt while also engaging culture as an integral part of her argument. After the prompt, you will find the excerpt of Martinez's writing that addresses the intersection of her topic (zombies in *The Walking Dead*) with its cultural significance in Atlanta.

Instructor Temple's "Zombies!" prompt:

What manifestation of zombies/living dead is the scariest? You may select from books, short stories, movies, television shows, comic books, or video games. Some questions to consider in making your selection are: What do the zombies look like? Are they human-like? Do they have any special abilities that set them apart from their human counterparts? In the world of the fiction you are analyzing, how are zombies created (by bites only or some other way)? How can the zombies be "killed"? What is the setting? (For example, is it realistic, futuristic, post-apocalyptic?) And, of course, how do you define "monster"?

Excerpt from Jessica Martinez's essay:

[Because of the show's realistic setting in present-day Georgia] where life is turned upside down, it may have a greater effect on local viewers. ["Walkers" could significantly frighten residents from Georgia because they are familiar with many of the buildings and towns where the walkers are shown.] Interestingly, the show is set in both the city and rural country, which demonstrates that humans cannot hide or escape from the flesh-craving walkers. The most frightening aspect of the zombies in *The Walking Dead* is the end of life as humans have come to know it. In a review about the show published in *Time* magazine, the author adds that "the more intriguing aspect of the series is the survivors and whether they can maintain a society worth surviving in. Which makes zombies an ideal metaphor…for our nightmares du jour: pandemics; decentralized terrorism; the collapse of social, financial and ecological systems" (Poniewozik). [Whenever an aspect in society challenges the status quo and lifestyle that people are accustomed to living, individuals tend to become frantic and frightened.]

Comment: Topic sentence transitions Martinez's argument about monsters into a consideration of place.

Comment: Notice how Martinez highlights the effect that cultural artifacts (buildings) and places (towns) have on viewers, particularly those with personal connections to the state.

Comment: Here we see how Martinez's narrow inquiry into a television show (i.e. cultural artifact) evokes a broader discussion about cultural behavior.

"Nostalgia" by Marissa Graziano

ENTRY POINT: CULTURE AND POLITICAL MODES OF INQUIRY

Once a writer establishes who, where, and what to research, she must then decide *how* to approach the research. Because the cultural writer engages the beliefs of a society in her writing, the argument produced about this society will always be **political**. The term **politics** is frequently used in popular culture to describe activities that relate to formal government operations, such as campaigning for elections and deliberating legislation.

However, the term *politics* itself extends beyond just government. Its etymology stems from the Greek word "polis," meaning city or society. In the most basic sense, *poli*tics refers to *any purpose that a person (or persons) endorse(s) within a society.* In this context, when a writer explores how a social trend influences or expresses culture, she engages politics in her argument because she writes about that social activity for a particular purpose.

The chart on page 175 outlines three common **political modes of inquiry** that can help shape your exploration of culture and further narrow the scope of your writing. This chart *is by no means a comprehensive list of all possible ways to inquire about a culture's politics.* Instead, it focuses on the key modes of inquiry in **identity politics**, or politics that pertain to the way individuals within a culture are identified, whether by themselves or by society as a whole. This chart also includes brainstorming questions

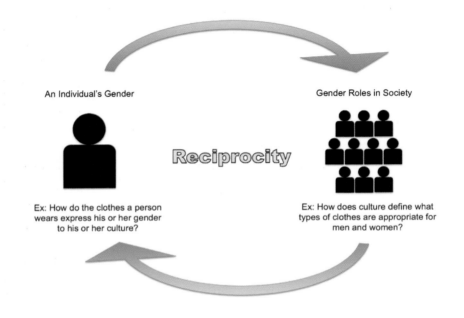

An Individual's Gender

Reciprocity

Gender Roles in Society

Ex: How do the clothes a person wears express his or her gender to his or her culture?

Ex: How does culture define what types of clothes are appropriate for men and women?

and sample research questions to help you apply these political modes of inquiry to your own writing.

POLITICAL MODES OF INQUIRY

Notice that in the "Political Modes of Inquiry" chart, each brainstorming question actually includes *two* questions. One asks how that particular identity category *influences* culture, and the other asks how culture *defines and produces* each identity category. This exchange of meaning between identity and culture demonstrates a **reciprocity** that is important to keep in

Political Modes of Inquiry	OED Definition	Potential Brainstorming Questions	Sample Research Questions
Race	"A group of people belonging to the same family and descended from a common ancestor; a house, family, kindred"	How does race inform social dynamics in the culture? How does the culture define or generate behavioral expectations for members of a particular race? How does that particular race define itself as conforming with or in opposition to the dominant culture?	How do race-based GSU student organizations interact with each other? What does their collaboration (or lack thereof) say about cultural beliefs about race among GSU undergraduate students today?
Gender	"Males or females viewed as a group; Also: the property or fact of belonging to one of these groups"	How do gender roles within this society shape broader social issues? How does this culture define and uphold gender roles?	Considering the dancing of college students at social gatherings, do the moves performed reveal anything about cultural expectations of gender? How might particular dance moves "perform" (or refuse to conform to) "acceptable" femininity or masculinity? How do they reveal what the culture expects from men and women?
Class	"A division or stratum of society consisting of people at the same economic level or having the same social status"	How does class organize social interactions? How does culture define or produce how class is expressed among members of the culture?	Considering fellow students at GSU, how does their parents' class status (low-income, middle-class, affluent) influence their selection of a major? What does this influence say about how different classes define a "successful" career?

mind when writing about culture. Race, gender, and class do not simply "exist" without social context; if they did, then people across all cultures around the world would believe and act the same way.

Because we know expressions and expectations of identity are *not* the same in every culture, the responsible cultural writer always keeps in mind that she is investigating a dynamic, reciprocal *relationship* between identity and culture, not a simple cause and effect.

CREATING A CULTURE-BASED RESEARCH QUESTION

When writing about culture, focusing on people, places, and artifacts is the best way to establish a research question that will focus your project. A **research question** is a way of turning a hypothesis or "hunch" about a given topic into a form that a writer can answer with research. The research question is a refined version of the broader topic. For example, a writer might choose to research Dr. Martin Luther King, Jr. for his essay on a social issue, but when he types in "Martin Luther King, Jr." in to the GSU Library's "Discover" search engine, it returns 236,143 results! He will need to narrow his topic in order to sort through this overwhelming volume of available sources.

Scope: Breadth and Depth

In order to focus his research question on Dr. King, our writer will need to narrow the *scope*, or focus, of his topic. A research scope can be measured in two ways:
- breadth, or how much material you can cover
- depth, or how thoroughly you can cover it

As a rule of thumb, most college courses expect a writer to favor depth over breadth, and just like in scientific research, a cultural writer must "control" for differences in variables to obtain a specific, supportable conclusion. In cultural work, the writer understands that the way a community in Capetown, South Africa remembers Dr. King is necessarily different than the way a community in Atlanta, Georgia remembers him, and residents in Dr. King's childhood neighborhood of Old Fourth Ward experience his memory still differently than, say, residents in Marietta.

To control for the differences in these geographic variables, a cultural writer will need to select the narrowest researchable scope possible so that he can go deeper into the topic than just the surface level. Recall that cultural writing engages the "ideas, customs, social behaviour, products, [and] way of life" for a community. Research about the ideas of a community compels the responsible writer to discover how individual members in that culture think and behave relative to the chosen topic. In order to research these thoughts thoroughly within the constraints of an assigned essay (typically five or more pages in length), a writer will need to narrow his scope.

Returning to the example given above, the original research topic of "Martin Luther King, Jr." was simply too broad; it returns *every topic* about Dr. King, in *every place* he influenced, in *every time period*. In cultural writing, asking brainstorming questions about the people, places, and artifacts related to your topic is a great way to narrow the scope and establish a research question. In the Dr. King example, the writer could ask himself the following four questions:

1. **PEOPLE:** Although my topic is a single person (Dr. King), my paper overall is a cultural project. And because a single person is not an entire culture, *which culture of people* am I interested in writing about relative to Dr. King?

Brainstorming Answers:

Politicians and/or activists during the Civil Rights Era

International diplomats who were/are influenced by Dr. King

Famous rhetoricians since Dr. King

Pop icons influenced by Dr. King

Writers (novelists, poets, screenwriters, playwrights)

His family

The "Everyday Joe" who remembers Dr. King's legacy

While all of the answers above might generate an intriguing essay, cultural writing privileges the everyday lived experience of members in a society—not only the political or popular figures in the media. Therefore, our writer might select the "Everyday Joe" in America, or the average American resident or citizen.

2. **PLACE:** Because my paper is about culture, *where* is the culture that Dr. King influenced?

Brainstorming Answers:

Throughout the World

In America

In the U.S. South

In his hometown of Atlanta

<u>In the neighborhood where he was born and reared: Old Fourth Ward</u>

While it is true that Dr. King influenced lives worldwide and throughout America, these places are too large to presume that all of the residents within them are part of the same culture, and there are too many people to perform thorough research. Turning to the U.S. South and Atlanta, while these are narrower than the first two options, they still include such a diversity of cultures that it would be difficult to cover all of them thoroughly within the length requirements of most college essays. There-fore, our writer will likely choose the narrowest researchable scope pos-sible: Old Fourth Ward.

3. **ARTIFACT(S) / ARCHIVE:** *What kind of materials* can produce the most information about the culture of the Old Fourth Ward neighborhood relative to Dr. King?

Brainstorming Answers:

Interviews with residents

Documented observation of the neighborhood

Objects located within the neighborhood

<u>Martin Luther King, Jr. National Park: exhibits and monuments</u>

Our writer must consider his time constraints and safety when deciding what materials he can use for his research. Because the National Park of-fers such a wealth of artifacts, and because it is safe, accessible, and can be surveyed within the time constraints of his assignment, the cultural writer might select this archive.

4. **POLITICAL MODE OF INQUIRY:** Given the people, place, and archive that I have selected, which political perspective is most relevant to my writing?

Brainstorming Answer:

Because Dr. King dedicated his life to activism in racial equality, and particularly because his greatest legacy in the American memory is as a champion of civil liberties, our writer is likely to select "race" as a productive mode of inquiry.

By funneling his topic through questions about people, place, artifacts/archives, and political modes of inquiry, our writer now has a narrower scope: "What can the exhibits and monuments at the Martin Luther King, Jr. National Park tell us about Dr. King's influence on the everyday person currently living in Atlanta's Old Fourth Ward neighborhood?" With a more focused research question, our writer is ready to get to work on his project.

Funnel Exercise

Narrowing down a topic into a research question is much like running sand through a funnel: it limits the volume that passes through while directing it in a neater, more organized manner. Take a moment to review the "funnel" diagrams below.

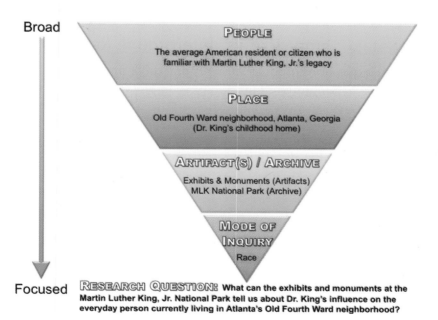

Broad

PEOPLE
The average American resident or citizen who is familiar with Martin Luther King, Jr.'s legacy

PLACE
Old Fourth Ward neighborhood, Atlanta, Georgia (Dr. King's childhood home)

ARTIFACT(S) / ARCHIVE
Exhibits & Monuments (Artifacts)
MLK National Park (Archive)

MODE OF INQUIRY
Race

Focused **RESEARCH QUESTION:** What can the exhibits and monuments at the Martin Luther King, Jr. National Park tell us about Dr. King's influence on the everyday person currently living in Atlanta's Old Fourth Ward neighborhood?

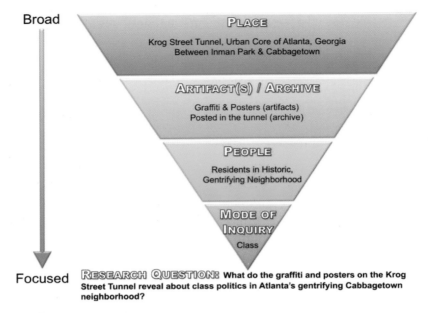

Broad

PLACE

Krog Street Tunnel, Urban Core of Atlanta, Georgia
Between Inman Park & Cabbagetown

ARTIFACT(S) / ARCHIVE

Graffiti & Posters (artifacts)
Posted in the tunnel (archive)

PEOPLE

Residents in Historic,
Gentrifying Neighborhood

MODE OF INQUIRY

Class

Focused RESEARCH QUESTION: **What do the graffiti and posters on the Krog Street Tunnel reveal about class politics in Atlanta's gentrifying Cabbagetown neighborhood?**

The first has been completed using the Martin Luther King, Jr. example above, and the next considers the Krog Street Tunnel example from earlier in this chapter. Notice that each starts with a different "entry point"—people, place, or artifact. When generating ideas for cultural writing, any of these categories may inspire your topic.

What's at Stake: Empirical vs. Interpretive Research

Cultural research questions produce answers that differ from those in other disciplines in that they are more *interpretive* than *empirical*. For example, in 2013, Jeremy Diem, an associate professor in GSU's Department of Geosciences, published his research on the effects of the Clean Air Act of 1970 in Atlanta, Georgia (for more information, see GSU's News webpage at http://news.gsu.edu/2013/06/05/research-clean-air-act-increased-atlanta-rainfall/). For Diem's scientific study, he asked the research question "Has rainfall in the Atlanta metropolitan area changed since the Clean Air Act was implemented? If so, in what way?" Notice that, just like in culture-based writing, Diem's scientific research question has a discrete scope: he is *only* measuring rainfall, *only* in the Atlanta metro area, and *only* since 1970. However, because this question can be unequivocally proven through scientific testing and observation, the answer he produces is *empirical*. The data resulting from Diem's research provides an answer that is, for the most part, self-evident: the rainfall increased, decreased, or remained the same.

In contrast, a cultural writer might use empirical evidence to contextualize and support his studies, but such empirical data would not be the intended result of his research question. Instead, he could ask, "how has the increase in rainfall caused by the Clean Air Act influenced the emergence of urban gardening culture?" Again, the scope of this culture-based research question is just as focused as its scientific sibling: he is *only* researching urban gardening as a cultural phenomena, *only* in the Atlanta urban core, and *only* since the Clean Air Act. However, this culture-based research question differs in the kind of conclusion it generates. Rather than concrete, empirical facts, the cultural writer uncovers the *ideology* that shapes the way members of a society interact with one another.

Unlike public policy or meteorological change, *ideology*—or the system of beliefs that organizes one's culture—is something that exists in the thoughts and opinions of members within that culture. And because thoughts and opinions cannot be scientifically tested, research questions about culture often lead to *interpretive* conclusions. For example, a researcher may interview urban Atlanta residents about their participation in and opinion of urban gardening relative to the increase in rainfall, but the answers given by a variety of interviewees will necessarily differ. A cultural writer's job is to identify any commonalities or systematic differences between the responses given and to *interpret* them for his readers.

A Reminder about Ethics in Cultural Writing

Because cultural writers are responsible for interpreting the opinions and experiences of others, they must approach their work with the utmost respect for the members of the cultures in discussion. For this reason, **we strongly recommend that you consider writing about a culture to which you already belong**. (See the "Doing the Right Thing" text box earlier in this chapter for more on the ethical considerations of cultural writing.)

CONCLUSION

No matter which entry point or political mode of inquiry you choose to practice writing through culture, developing a focused research question with a narrow scope is a fundamental step to organizing your research and writing in English 1101 or 1102. Each of these cultural gateways can be explored through the writing heuristics and research techniques you have already learned in Chapters 1-5 in order to compose an essay that engages the world around you. When you choose to write about culture, you seize the moment to understand not only culture itself, but also your relationship to it. Most importantly, you can take the timely opportunity to improve political issues for that community. Whether your goal is to inform your reader about a little-known issue or to propose a change in the way a culture operates, you will engage a topic that matters beyond the limits of your classroom. You are writing with a purpose; you are engaging praxis.

Index

Q

R

S

NOTES

NOTES

NOTES

NOTES

NOTES

NOTES

NOTES

NOTES

NOTES